FreeStuff

FOR

Traveling
Quilters
ON THE INTERNET

GLORIA HANSEN

C&T PUBLISHING

Developmental Editor: Barbara Kuhn
Copy Editor: Lucy Grijalva
Cover and Book Design: Christina Jarumay
Travel Icon Illustrations: Stephanie Muir
Illustration: Claudia Böhm
Book Production: Nancy Koerner
Production Assistant: Stephanie Muir

Library of Congress Cataloging-in-Publication Data

Hansen, Gloria.
   Free stuff for traveling quilters on the Internet / Gloria Hansen.
      p.   cm.
   ISBN 1-57120-122-X
   1. Quilting--Computer network resources. 2. Travel--
Computer network resources--Directories. 3. Internet addresses--
Directories. 4. Web sites--Directories 5. Free material--Computer
network resources--Directories. I. Title.
II. Title.
   TT835 .H3359 2000
   025.06'74646--dc21

                                        00-011789

Published by C&T Publishing, Inc.
P.O. Box 1456
Lafayette, California 94549

82624

Printed in China
10   9   8   7   6   5   4   3   2   1

DEDICATION

To Judy Heim. Thank you for encouraging me to write this book.

ACKNOWLEDGEMENTS

My deepest thanks to all of the quilters and travelers who share so generously of themselves and their wisdom on the Web. Without you, this book would not be possible.

A special thanks to Susan Adler, Jinny Beyer, Marty Bowne, MaryAnn Burns, Nancy Crow, Judy B. Dales, Carol Doak, Nancy Eha, Ann Fahl, Susan B. Faeder, Caryl Bryer Fallert, Rob and Lynn Holland, Judy Mathieson, Carol Miller, Dian (E/Less) Moore, Norma McKone, Sarah Patrowicz, Yvonne Porcella, Susan (Lucky) Shie, Judy Smith, Nancy Schlegel, Kathy Schmidt, Andi Stern, John Swiatek, and Joen Wolfrom, for graciously sharing their travel advice and wisdom.

My final thanks to Barb Kuhn, Christina Jarumay, Lucy Grijalva, Lynn Koolish, Nancy Koerner, and the team at C&T Publishing.

DEAR READER,

Sifting through the sites to create this book was a challenge. My goal was to include sites that will be updated with fresh information and offer the best advice and guidance for traveling quilters. That doesn't mean, however, there aren't many more sites out there that are equally illuminating and valuable; you may find others. Given the fluid nature of the Web, it is possible that some of the sites in this book may move or even vanish. Even so, I believe this book gives you the tools to navigate the vast, ever-evolving world of the Web. Enjoy the journey. —Gloria

---

SYMBOLS IN THIS BOOK

 This icon represents travel wisdom and advice shared by an esteemed quiltmaker.

 This icon signifies noteworthy advice.

 When you see this icon, read carefully. It represents hard-earned wisdom—something I learned the hard way.

 This icon tells you that the Web site sells merchandise related to the free information on the site.

Table of Contents

traveling Quilters
Love the Web!

Quilters are special people—they create beauty and warmth and are always eager to share and learn. Quilters are a friendly bunch with an adventurous spirit, spontaneously getting together with pals, and venturing off practically anywhere to see a quilt show, take a quilt class, or meet up with other quilters for some fun. Traveling quilters love the Web because it's a gateway to quilters worldwide. And a place where free information and answers reign. Do you wonder if there are good quilting stores in western Pennsylvania? What attractions you should see while in Williamsburg? When Quilt Festival is this year? How you can get an entry form to Quilt National? If anyone wants to join you on a quilting cruise or room with you at a symposium? No matter what questions you have, chances are you'll find answers on the Web—and this book shows you how.

THIS BOOK HELPS YOU LOCATE THE BEST FREE INFORMATION FOR YOUR QUILTING ADVENTURES AND TRAVEL NEEDS

The Web is a huge, ever-growing, indispensable resource—a boon for traveling quilters. But its plethora of unorganized sites may feel overwhelming, and you often need plenty of perseverance to find what you're looking for. Using a search engine can turn up thousands of sites—a mosaic of both the helpful and unhelpful, and often not the most useful. With this book in hand, you will save valuable time by quickly locating the best sites for your quilting adventure and travel needs. Let the Web empower you, not overwhelm you. Use this book to get on the Web and find:

- The biggest and best general travel sites where you'll find feature stories, articles, travel bargains, and family travel ideas.
- Web sites with directories to local and world-wide quilt shops.
- Web sites where you can find all of the latest quilting show and contest news, plus information on quilting retreats, cruises, and tours.
- Web sites with directories of festivals and fairs, arts and crafts schools, and museums.
- Web sites to help you locate your favorite quilting teachers and their current schedules.
- Web sites with updated listings for guilds located throughout the world.
- Web sites where you can talk to other quilters, post your traveling questions, ask opinions on shows, and find advice on the best shopping.
- Web sites to help you find all the tourist information you need.
- Web sites with international travel help and guidance.
- Web sites that will help keep you connected on the road.

While this book is geared to wanderlust quilters, others looking for travel adventure will find valuable information and ideas, too.

WHAT YOU NEED TO GET ON THE WEB

If you're buying a new computer, you're in luck. Almost all computers sold today come with the necessary hardware and software to get you on the Web. Here's what you need:

- A computer (one that can at least run Windows 95 or Mac OS System 7.5).
- An internal or external modem (56K BPS is the minimum recommended speed).
- A telephone line.
- An Internet Service Provider (ISP)—the company that will provide you with Internet access.
- A browser—the software you use to view the Web (such as Netscape Navigator or Internet Explorer).

▲ AMERICA ONLINE
🜨 IS PERFECT FOR BEGINNERS

America Online is a commercial online service that offers original content and a gateway to the Internet. It's very easy to install, making it a great choice for beginners. If you are not one of the many who have received an AOL special offer CD in the mail or found one falling from the pages of a favorite magazine, you can request a free AOL installation CD by calling 1-800/827-6364. Or, if you know someone with Internet access, you can ask them to download a copy of the software from AOL's Web site (**http://www.aol.com**). AOL offers different pricing plans, from $4.95 for limited monthly access to $21.95 for unlimited access.

To install AOL on your computer, load the CD, click the install icon, and follow the instructions. The program helps locate your closest access number (the number your program will dial to get you online) and configures your computer settings (great for those who'd rather not tinker with settings). Within a very short time, you're online hearing "welcome." While online, take the tour to understand how AOL works and what it offers. You'll quickly discover why AOL has millions of subscribers—it's fun and offers plenty of organized, easy-to-follow content.

In addition to AOL's fees, there may be surcharges. If there is no local access number in your area, your options are to use the next closest number, and be charged for long distance calls by your telephone company. If you use an AOL 800 access number, it adds a $6.00 per hour surcharge to your monthly bill.

▲ AOL
🜨 KEYWORDS

▼ travel		Go	Search	Keyword

Keywords are shortcuts that allow you to jump to different places on AOL. To access AOL's travel area using a keyword, type **travel** into the white navigation box on AOL's toolbar (where it says, "Type Search words, Keywords or Web Addresses here"), and click the **go** button.

You can also type keywords into AOL's keyword box. Click the keyword box icon on the navigation toolbar to access it, or press Ctrl-K (or ⌘ -K on a Mac).

✋ *Sometimes it's confusing when you type in what you think is an AOL keyword, and the browser window pops open and whisks you off to the Web. This is because keywords can also be used in place of long Web addresses or to start an Internet search. An easy way to know whether you're in AOL or on the Web is to look at the white navigation box on AOL's toolbar. If it has a URL address in it (for example:* (**http://www.somewhereontheWeb.com**)*, you're on the Web. If it says "Type Search words, Keywords or Web Addresses here," you're still in AOL.*

🛍 TIPS FOR FINDING TRAVEL AND QUILTING ADVICE ON AMERICA ONLINE

To access AOL's travel area, type the Keyword: **Travel**. Since travel is such a popular topic on AOL, you can also quickly access it by clicking the **Travel** button on the lower left of your Welcome screen.

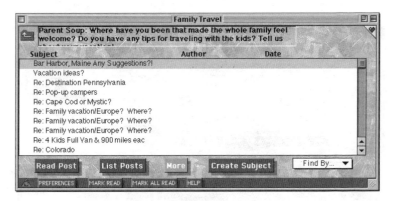

To chat with other travelers, select Travelers' Opinions. Because certain travel options are accessible to the public through the Web, anything from AOL's travel channel launches AOL's Web browser and opens the travel page.

The message boards are an AOL-only feature. Selecting "family travel" opens the AOL Family Travel message board. You can toggle back and forth between AOL-only content and AOL's Web browser window.

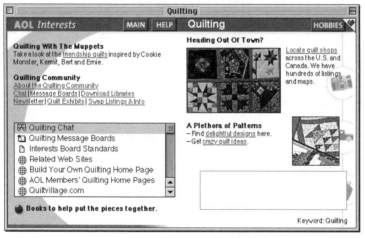

This Week's Chat Schedule

Shore Excursions
Saturday, 9 pm ET

Add a chat to your personal event calendar: Click Here

Sunday
Disney Hour   10:00 pm ET
First Time Cruisers: 9:00 pm ET
Monday
Caribbean Travel: 8:30 pm ET
The Cruise Experience: 9:00 pm ET
National Parks: 10:00 pm ET
Tuesday
European Traveler: 9:00 pm ET
Cruise Chatter: 9:00 pm ET

Promote your business without leaving your desk.

Camping Chats. Open 24 hours a day. Drop by for a visit!

AOL also offers regular travel chats. To access them, select Chats from the Travelers' Opinions page. To join a chat, follow the online instructions.

Quilting With The Muppets
Take a look at the friendship quilts inspired by Cookie Monster, Kermit, Bert and Ernie.

Quilting Community
About the Quilting Community
Chat | Message Boards | Download Libraries
Newsletter | Quilt Exhibits | Swap Listings & Info

Quilting Chat
Quilting Message Boards
Interests Board Standards
Related Web Sites
Build Your Own Quilting Home Page
AOL Members' Quilting Home Pages
Quiltvillage.com

Books to help put the pieces together.

Heading Out Of Town?
Locate quilt shops across the U.S. and Canada. We have hundreds of listings and maps.

A Plethora of Patterns
– Find delightful designs here.
– Get crazy quilt ideas.

Keyword: Quilting

Type the Keyword: **Quilting** to tap into AOL's quilting interest area.

Quilting Fun		

Welcome to Quilting Message boards. Before posting, please review the AOL Hobbies Guidelines.

Topics	Subjects
*** Quilt Forum Announcements ***	1
*** Quilt Forum Suggestion Box ***	0
AOL Qltrs Get-togethers	1
Ask QuiltS is about the Quilt Forum	4
Chats	5
Contests & Challenges	0
Current Quilt Project	23
Internet	2
Introduce yourself	37
Kids 'n Quilting	8
Labels & Poetry	0
Local Guild News	10

List All **List Unread** **Mark Read** **More** **Subscribe** Find By...

ABOUT MESSAGE BOARDS   PREFERENCES   HELP

In the quilting area you'll find several active message boards. To find them, select "Message Boards" under Quilting Community. A small dialog box will appear with message board guidelines and three quilting boards to choose from—quilting fun, serious quilting, and not just quilts.

On AOL or the Web?

The white navigation box on the AOL toolbar indicates whether you are on AOL or off on the Web.

Type Search words, Keywords or Web Addresses here   Go "Search Keyword

If you see "Type Search words, Keywords or Web Addresses here" in the white box, you're on AOL.

http://www.quiltingbythelake.com/welcome.html   Go Search Keyword

If you see a URL address, such as **http://www.quiltingbythelake.com**, you're on the Web.

HOW TO USE AMERICA ONLINE'S WEB BROWSER

To jump from AOL to a Web site, you simply need to type the Web site's URL (Uniform Resource Locator—the Web site's address) into the white navigation box on AOL's toolbar and click the **go** button.

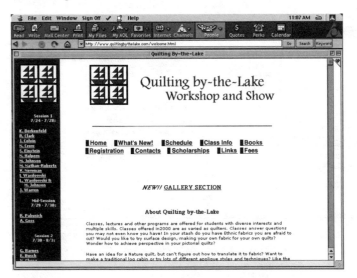

For example, if you type <**http://www.quiltingbythelake.com**>, you'll be connected to the Quilting by the Lake's Web site.

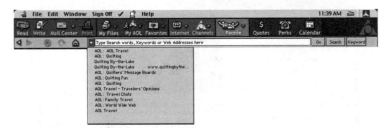

To jump from the Web site back to a favorite place you visited on AOL, mouse-click and hold on the arrow button to the left of the white navigation box on the toolbar. This will display a drop-down menu that lists the last 25 places you visited—either on the Web or on AOL. Simply select your favorite place from this list.

T I P

Learn More About AOL and AOL Safety Tips.

While connected to AOL, start with Keyword: **Help** for a good overview of the service. Keyword: **Customer Service** provides information on 24 hour help services and keywords to other helpful areas.

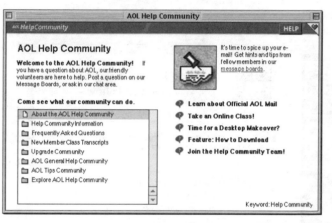

*Head to Keyword: **Help Community** for message boards loaded with excellent tech support, free online classes on AOL and the Internet, and plenty of hints and tips.*

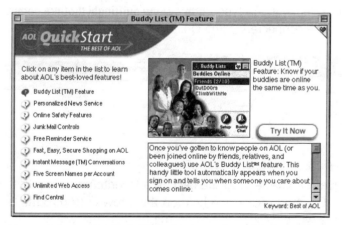

*Keyword: **Best of AOL** is filled with tips and tutorials for using AOL's most popular features, such as the Buddy List and Instant Message conversations.*

Visit Keyword: **Neighborhood Watch** for information on parental controls, e-mail safety, computer safety, and suggested safeguards.

Never give any personal information, such as your password or credit card numbers, to anyone. If you receive a request for any personal information, do not respond. Instead, report it to AOL. See Keyword: **Notify** for guidance.

AOL only sends its Official Mail to users within a blue envelope with a blue border that includes the official AOL seal. When you view the e-mail, you'll notice a light-blue border behind the mail buttons, and the official AOL seal located on the lower left corner of the mail border. Note that AOL will never ask you for your password or other personal information.

MORE AMERICA ONLINE TIPS

Turning off Web graphics: Some sites have so many images that, depending on your connection speed, you can wait a long time for the page to load. If you are only interested in reading the information, you can turn the images off. Head over to the **My AOL** icon on the AOL navigation toolbar and select **Preferences**. Select the **WWW** button from the left column. Uncheck the **Show Images** check box and click **OK**. Should you want to see an image while at a Web site, simply double-click on the box for the image and it will load.

Emptying your Cache: The Web browser cache stores the HTML and graphics of a site you visited on your hard drive. This speeds things up when you return to a site while you're still logged on. But performance slows down when the cache fills up. To empty AOL's browser cache, go to the **My AOL** icon on the AOL navigation toolbar and select **Preferences**. Select the **WWW** button from the left column. Click the **Empty Cache Now** button, and click **OK**.

Using a different browser: Most people prefer to use Netscape Navigator or Internet Explorer to view Web pages instead of AOL's browser. Using a different browser while in AOL is simple: Once connected to AOL, minimize the AOL window (Mac users can close the window) and launch your favorite.

TIP

Mac Users Try John Moe's **Net Print** (**http://www93.pair.com/johnmoe**). This $10 shareware program allows you to highlight any text in your browser window (and other programs, too) and print or save it.

HOW TO SHOP FOR OTHER INTERNET SERVICE PROVIDERS

If you don't want to use America Online (and many people don't), look for an ISP. Currently there are thousands to select from, and finding the right ISP often becomes a daunting task. Ask friends, co-workers, or neighbors for their recommendations. Find out why certain providers are liked or disliked. And use the following guidelines:

• Look for an ISP with a fast connection (T1 or better, directly into the Internet's network) and 56K bps connections that support the same connection standards as your modem.

• Inquire about technical support. Your ISP should help configure your browser (or provide you with software that will configure it for you) and be available around the clock to answer any questions you may have.

• Find out how long the company has been in business (four years or more is good), and how many customers it has (organizations in addition to individuals). If it's a local provider, ask for customer references and call to find out what they like and dislike about their service.

• Monthly fees should be about $20 per month, include unlimited connection time, 56K bps connections, free Web page hosting, and free e-mail.

Favorite national Internet Service Providers include Earthlink (**http://www.earthlink.net)**, and AT&T WorldNet (**http://www.att.net**). For help locating an ISP to meet your needs and budget, visit The List (**http://www.thelist.com**).

HIGH SPEED INTERNET ACCESS THROUGH CABLE AND DSL

There was a time when only certain businesses were able to obtain high-speed Internet access. For the rest of us, the keyword was wait. Wait for the service to dial-up and connect. Wait for e-mail messages to appear. Wait for a Web page to load. And downloads? That was anything from a watch-a-sitcom wait to a walk around the block wait. Today, fast home Internet access is increasing as cable and digital subscription line modems (DSL) are being offered in many—alas, not all—areas of the country. Both services are digital, not analog. That means there are no annoying dial-up sounds, and the service is connected twenty four hours a day, seven days a week. You need only launch your browser to be online.

Cable. The same two-way cable that brings cable television into your house can also handle high-speed data connections. The best way to find out whether cable Internet is available in your area is to call your local cable company. Some communities have only one-way cable for signals to come into your home. If you live in such a community, you'll have to wait for your cable company to first upgrade to coaxial (or two-way) cable before Internet access will be available.

If your cable company does offer an Internet connection, ask if there are any special deals. My installation was free because the company was running a promotion. A typical installation is about $150–200—and make sure you thoroughly test-drive your connection before allowing the technician to leave your house. Monthly fees are about $40–50, depending on whether you also have cable television from the same provider.

When I first subscribed to cable Internet, I had an incredibly fast connection as the service was new and not many subscribed. As cable Internet became popular in my town, my connection speed s-l-o-w-e-d, especially during peak hours of use. Why? Because a cable Internet connection is similar to a party telephone line (remember those?). It's a shared line. The more people on, the more congested and the slower rate of data flow. If this happens to you, keep calling your cable company to complain. Also request that a signal be sent to your modem to confirm that it's properly set. My connection is speedy again. How speedy? I recently downloaded the latest version of American Online in 4 minutes. The estimated download time for a 56k bps modem was 28 minutes; 28K bps: 56 minutes; and 14.4K bps: 1 hour and 52 minutes.

DSL. Also referred to as a digital subscription line, DSL allows fast Internet connections to homeowners (and small businesses) over a telephone line. Amazingly, it does not interfere with a normal telephone call. You can talk on the phone at the same time you sift through Web sites.

To find out if DSL is available in your area, call your local telephone company. It will determine where its nearest digital center is, if you reside within three miles of it, and whether your phone lines can handle the data flow. If you pass the tests, consider your keyword lucky. If you choose to proceed, some companies provide free installation and others charge anywhere from $150 to $350 (again, check for promotions). Monthly fees for average home users can range $40-70 per month (small business plans are higher). While the cost is generally higher than cable, DSL has a clear advantage—a dedicated line. The line is only yours, meaning a steady and predictable rate of speed starting at about ten times faster than a 56K bps connection.

For more information on cable and DSL Internet access, see **Cable Modem Info (http://www.cablemodeminfo.com)**, **Cable Modem Help (http://www.cablemodemhelp.com)**, **Cable Modem Network (http://www.cable-modem.net)**, **DLS Forum (http://www.adsl.com)**, and **Everything DSL (http://www.everythingdsl.com)** which includes warnings about free DSL scams. Internet cable or DSL users running **Windows 98/NT** can visit **Speed Tweaks (http://www.cable-modems.org/ articles/speed_tweaks)** to fine-tune your Windows registry and improve your connection speed.

SATELLITE CABLE ACCESS

While not as fast as cable or DSL, connecting to a satellite Internet service can be up to eight times faster than a 56K bps modem connection. For starters, you need a Pentium PC with Windows 95 or better, a 28.8K bps (or faster) modem, 32 MB of RAM, and 100 MB of hard disk space. Next you need to install a receiver dish antenna (cost about $200 to $400) and you must have a direct unobstructed line-of-sight to the satellite (which in New Jersey means the southwest). Although you can align the dish yourself, it's probably worth the additional couple hundred dollars to pay someone who knows what he/she is doing. Unfortunately, even after everything is up and running smoothly, bad weather can knock the dish out of whack and prompt a service call. In areas where cable and DSL are not available, satellite service is an option to Windows users wanting a faster connection. Different pricing plans are available ranging from $19.95 to $129.95 per month, without ISP. For more information, see Hughes Network System's **DirecPC** (**http://www.direcpc.com**), the country's leading satellite Internet service provider.

ISP Users Who Also Want AOL Can Save Money.

If you want an ISP and AOL, or if you have ISP access through work, school, or a high-speed Internet connection and you want an AOL account too, sign up for AOL's Bring Your Own Access (BYOA) plan. It allows you unlimited connection through your ISP for $9.95 per month instead of AOL's usual $21.95 per month. If you currently have an AOL account and want to change to BYOA, type keyword **Billing** and follow the instructions. Note that if you have BYOA and sign on to AOL as a guest from someone else's AOL access number account, you will incur a ten cents per minute surcharge.

▟ WHAT TRAVELING QUILTERS NEED TO KNOW ABOUT BROWSERS

No matter what Internet service you use, in order to view the Web you need a browser. Years ago you also needed separate programs for doing other things on the Internet, such sending and retrieving e-mail, participating in Usenet newsgroups, or downloading files. Today's browsers have simplified things by including all these features. The two most popular browsers are Netscape Navigator (or Communicator, a larger suite of programs with Navigator being the browser) and Microsoft's Internet Explorer. Both are free.

While your ISP will supply you with a browser, chances are you already have one installed on your hard drive. You do not have to use the browser that came with your computer. Use whatever you wish, including text-only browsers or other browsers such as AOL's. Many people regularly alternate between them.

Configuring your browser can be tricky. Make sure your ISP helps set up your browser or provides you with software that configures it for you. Once configured, copy the settings (located in the TCP/IP control panel) and keep them in a safe place.

▟ HOW AND WHY YOU SHOULD KEEP YOUR BROWSER CURRENT

Most people happily use a particular program because it's easier than having to upgrade. However, it's important that you keep your browser up-to-date. Besides being compatible with the latest developments in Internet technology, using the latest version also keeps your computer secure by fixing whatever security holes needed patching.

You can find out what version of Netscape you have by pulling down the Help menu and selecting **About Navigator** (or **About Communicator**, depending on what's installed). If it's less than version 4.7, upgrade. Click the **Netscape** icon in the Navigation Toolbar (if you don't see it, select **View/Show/Navigation Toolbar** from the menu) or head over to **Netscape** (**http://www.netscape.com**) and select **download**. A smart-download feature is available that may help speed up your download process.

Click the Netscape icon in the Navigation Toolbar to go directly to Netscape's Web page. From there, click download.

You can learn what version of Internet Explorer you have by pulling down the Help menu and selecting **About Internet Explorer**. Upgrade if it's less than version 5.0. Click the **IE** icon on the far right of the button bar to go to Microsoft's IE download page (if you don't see it, select **View/Button Bar** from the menu). Windows users can access the page by typing **<http://www.microsoft.com/windows/ie/download>** and Macintosh users can access the page by typing **<http://www.microsoft.com/mac/products/ie>**.

Click the Internet Explorer icon on the far right of the button bar to go directly to Microsoft's IE download page.

WEB ACCESS FOR OLDER COMPUTERS

To get Internet access, you don't need a new computer. Even those with an original Apple II, circa 1979, can tap in. But to view graphics, you'll need a computer manufactured within the last 8 years.

Opera (**http://www.opera.com**) is an inexpensive browser that includes news and e-mail. In addition to being a browser alternative to the big two (Netscape and Explorer), it works without a hitch on a 486 PC with 8 MB of RAM and Windows 3.1— and it can work on older systems too. A Mac version of Opera may be available by the time you read this.

If you're running an older Macintosh (even a black/white Mac), head to Chris Adams' **Web Browser for Antique Macs** Web page (**http://www.edprint.demon.co.uk/se/macWeb.html**). Chris offers an informative page detailing which browser is best to use with your Mac and includes downloads for Tradewave's MacWeb, NCSA Mosaic, early versions of Netscape, and others.

▞▚ HOW TO ACCESS
▞▚ A WEB PAGE

Now that your browser is ready, it's time to surf the Web.

Address: @ http://www.jinnybeyer.com/

To access a Web page, type the Web site's address (commonly called **URL** or "Uniform Resource Locator") into the white window bar—called **Location** in Netscape or **Address** in IE—and press **Enter** (**Return** on a Mac). For example, to access Jinny Beyer's Web site, type **<http://www.jinnybeyer.com>**.

> ✋ *Because each address is unique, it's extremely important that URLs are typed exactly as they appear. If you're missing a single letter, a punctuation mark, or using a lower-case letter instead of an upper-case letter, the Web browser will not be able to locate the desired page.*

You can cut and paste URLs from other documents into the location or address bar. Use your mouse to highlight the address. Then press Ctrl-C (⌘-**C** on a Mac) to copy the address. Use your mouse to click onto the location or address bar, highlight any current address in the box, and press Ctrl-V (⌘-**V** on a Mac) to paste in the new address. Then press **Enter** (**Return** on a Mac).

TIP

Sites starting with **http://** are so common that newer browsers don't require you to type that portion of the URL. For example, if you type **<www.jinnybeyer.com>** into your location or address window, your browser will automatically insert **http://** and whisk you to Jinny Beyer's site.

HOW TO NAVIGATE THE WEB WITHOUT GETTING LOST

When viewing Web pages, you'll notice certain words that are underlined and in a color different from the rest of the text. These words are known as **hyperlinks**, links, or hotlinks. By clicking on a link, you are transported to a new Web site— either a new page on the site you're visiting or an entirely different site. You can easily jump from Web site to Web site (also called "surfing" the Web) by clicking on links. Often images are links to other sites, too. With so much jumping from site to site, you may find yourself lost and wanting to get back to some earlier sites that you visited. Here's how:

*Click the **Back** button on the Navigation or Button bar to return to the previous Web site (or **Go/Back** from the menu).*

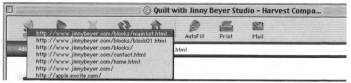

*Right-click (click-hold on a Mac) on the **Back** button to display a drop-down list of Web sites you recently visited. To return to a site, simply select it. Selecting **Go** from the menu displays a similar drop-down menu.*

In Internet Explorer, selecting **GO** from the menu will also display a day-by-day history of the sites you visited (or you can select **Window/History** from the menu bar). To change the number of sites saved or to clear the history, select **Edit/Preferences** from the menu. A dialog box will appear. Select **Web Browser** in the left column, and select **Advanced**. In the History portion of the dialog box, edit the **Places Visited** box or click the **Clear History** button.

To display **History** information in Netscape Navigator, select **Communicator/Tools/History** from the menu. To change how long Web pages are tracked in the History window or to clear the History, select **Edit/Preferences** from the menu. A dialog box will appear. Select Navigator from the left column. Type in the number of days in the box or click the **Expire Now** button to clear the history. Note that on the Mac OS, page visits are only recorded for the current session and will expire when you quit the application.

TIP

THE ANATOMY
OF A WEB ADDRESS

A **URL** (Uniform Resource Locator) is the unique address that takes you to a specific Internet site. The first couple letters in the address (called the URL prefix) indicate what type of Internet site you're connecting to. The most common prefix is **http**, which stands for "hypertext transfer protocol" and is used for transferring files; **news**, for connecting to a newsgroup; and **mailto**, for displaying an outgoing e-mail window.

The URL prefix is always followed by a colon and two slashes **://**. This punctuation separates the prefix from the document's address. The most common URL addresses are to sites located on the World Wide Web. They start **http://www**. Following the **www** is a period, referred to as dot, and used to separate different sections of the Web address. Next comes the domain name, the entity that runs the site. Common suffixes include **.com** (commercial), **.edu** (university), **.org** (non-profit organization), and **.gov** (government). For example, <**http://www.jinnybeyer.com**> is a commercial site on the Wide World Web.

The pages (or documents) that make up a Web site are stored either on the domain name site or in directories or subdirectories of the site (depending on the site's organization—and similar to the directory path on your computer). Each slash of a URL represents a directory. The more slashes, the more subdirectories. The document name of a particular page is located after the last slash and generally ends with **.html** or **.htm**. In <**http://www.jinnybeyer.com/home.html**> "home.html" is a document on the jinnybeyer.com site.

HOW TO SEARCH FOR WEB SITES

If you're trying to locate information, the Internet is the place to look. But with its seemingly gazillion pages of information and absolutely no type of centralized organization system (imagine an unalphabetized phone book), locating what you're looking for can be like finding the proverbial needle in a haystack. If you're faced with a "Not Found" error message for a site you seek, or if you're looking for more information, try an Internet search service. Here's an overview:

Directory. Perfect for looking for general information on a particular topic, directory services' employ people to view individual sites and classify worthy pages into subject category and subcategory schemes. Yahoo! (**http://www.yahoo.com**), LookSmart (**http://www.looksmart.com**), and InfoSpace (**http://www.infospace.com**) are three popular services.

Search Engine. It's what to use when looking for specific information on a topic. Its index of sites is mainly created by "spiders" or "bots" (short for robots) that visit Web sites and add whatever pages it finds into a large database. AltaVista (**http://www.altavista.com**) and Lycos (**http://www.lycos.com**) are two search engines, both of which also include directories. Because search engines primarily rely on spiders rather than people to gather information, far more Web sites are indexed in search engines than are found on directories.

Metasearch Engine. Use it to search multiple search sites with a single search. MetaCrawler (**http://www.metacrawler.com**), SavvySearch (**http://www.savvysearch.com**), and Dogpile (**http://www.dogpile.com**).

To use a search engine, enter a series of keywords in the designated window and click the "search" button. The engine will then search its database and present a list of links based on those keywords. It's not uncommon for a search to result in thousands of "hits" or "matches"—far too many to sort through. To get better search results, use quotation marks around keywords to search for exact phrases. Also, read the advanced search options at the search engine's site for additional advice on how you can narrow your search.

Ask Jeeves (**http://www.askjeeves.com**) is a different approach to a search engine. Instead of typing keywords, you type in a question and it presents sites that may answer.

T I P

Does Your Connection Seem SLOW?

• If your connection seems slow, check that your modem speed is properly set. If your software is set at a speed that's faster than your modem is capable of handling, things will slow down. If you're not sure what it should be set at, experiment by lowering the speed and testing to see if you get better performance. If you have no idea what your modem speed should be set at or how to reset it, call your ISP for help. If you have a cable Internet connection, call your provider and ask that a signal be sent to your modem to confirm that it's properly set.

• If you upgraded your browser and things seem slow, check the browser's minimum requirements. It's possible your computer may need more physical memory.

• The biggest reason for a slow connection speed is heavy traffic. Like hitting a crowded toll booth when coming off a highway, if there are too many people on the Internet, or trying to access the same site at the same time, things slow down. Peak traffic times are often late afternoon and early evening. Unfortunately, like real traffic, there's no way to avoid traffic unless you avoid rush hour.

HOW TO CREATE AN INTERNET SHORTCUT BY ADDING SITES TO YOUR WINDOWS OR MACINTOSH DESKTOP

If you have a favorite site that you visit daily, you can add a shortcut to it from your Windows 95 (or higher) or Mac desktop. If the page you want to add a shortcut to is loaded in Netscape, use your mouse to drag the bookmark icon (to the left of the URL location window) from the browser to your desktop (in Navigator, drag the icon located to the left of the URL). A shortcut icon will appear. By clicking the icon, your browser will launch, your ISP will connect, and you'll be whisked to the Web site.

HOW TO FIND A WEB SITE THAT'S MOVED

Web-site owners update their sites on a regular basis. Sometimes in the process of updating, a site is over-hauled with new directories and subdirectories. If this happens, the document you're looking for may have been moved or renamed and may not be in the place your URL points to. In this case, you will get a Not Found error message.

Try finding the page by deleting the last portion of the URL, working backwards to the slash. For example, Susan Druding offers a free subscription to a quilting newsletter at her site. The URL is <**http://quilting.about .com/hobbies/quilting/library/weekly/blQNuggt.htm**>. If you typed the URL and got a Not Found message, delete the "/blQNuggt.htm" portion of the URL and hit **Enter** (**Return** on a Mac). If there's nothing there or you get a strange error message, continue working back through the URL until you locate the page or find the domain name, where you can search the site and find the desired page.

For example, you can delete the last portion of the URL and go from:

http://quilting.about.com/hobbies/quilting/library/weekly/ blQNuggt.htm
   to
http://quilting.about.com/hobbies/quilting/library/weekly
   to
http://quilting.about.com/hobbies/quilting/library
   to
http://quilting.about.com/hobbies/quilting
   to
http://quilting.about.com/hobbies
   to
http://quilting.about.com

Sometimes when working back through the URL, you can arrive at a directory listing of files. If so, look for a file that ends with a .html or .htm and click on it. Both extensions indicate the file is a document (.gif and .jpg are image extensions). If you get an "Access Denied" message, try going further back through the URL.

 *Working back through a URL address can often help you to locate a page that has moved. But it doesn't mean the page still exists. Sometimes the site owner may move to a new domain. In that case, see "How to Search for Web Sites" earlier in this chapter. If the site owner deleted a page or deleted the entire site, then it's gone.*

Use Third-Party Software to Organize Your Bookmarks. If you love hordes of bookmarks and want to use them while in different browsers, consider a low-cost bookmark utility program. Such programs allow you to save and organize your bookmarks in a central location accessible by any browser. A good place to download them is from C/net's **Shareware.Com** (**http://www.shareware.com**). Search for the phrase "bookmark organizer." For PCs, try the $29 shareware program LinkMan Professional from Thomas Reimann. For Macs, try **URL Manager Pro**, the $25 shareware program from Alco Blom (**http://www.url-manager.com**).

HOW TO CREATE AND ORGANIZE BOOKMARKS

Web browsers let you "bookmark" sites. A bookmark allows your browser to revisit a selected site with a mouse-click rather than your having to retype the site's URL. Bookmarks are easy to create and use, and it's not difficult to amass a large quantity of bookmarks in a short period of time. Luckily browsers also allow you to organize and customize your bookmarks.

How to Add and Use a Bookmark

To add a bookmark in Navigator while you are viewing a site, click **Bookmarks** (Mac users select **Bookmarks/Add** from the menu). To add a bookmark to Explorer while you are viewing a site, select **Favorites/Add to Favorites** from the menu. Note that Explorer calls bookmarks "Favorites." You'll notice that both Navigator and Explorer come preloaded with a selection of bookmarks to sites they believe you'll enjoy visiting. To use a bookmark, simply click **Bookmark** or **Favorites** on the menu and select the site you want to visit.

To add a bookmark to Explorer while you are viewing a site, select Favorite/Add to Favorites from the menu.

Favorites	
Add Page to Favorites	⌘D
Organize Favorites	▶
Update Subscriptions	⌘U
Subscribe...	
🖻 **Toolbar Favorites**	▶
🖻 **Support and Information**	▶
@ **Quilting By-the-Lake ...... www.quiltingbythe...**	
🖻 **Quilting Sites**	▶
🖻 **Travel Sites**	▶

To use a bookmark in Explorer, click Favorites on the menu and select the site you want to visit.

How to Organize and Edit Bookmarks

To organize your bookmarks in Navigator, click the **Bookmarks** icon and select **Edit Bookmarks** (Mac users select **Bookmarks/Edit Bookmarks** from the menu). A dialog box appears with a list of your bookmarks. Click the item above where you want to place a new folder or a new dividing line. To add a folder, select **File/New Folder** from the menu; type a name for the folder and click OK. To add a separator, or dividing line, select **File/New Separator**. To edit bookmarks click the **Bookmarks** icon and select **Edit Bookmarks** (Mac users select **Bookmarks/Edit Bookmarks** from the menu. You can drag folders to reorder them, and delete folders or sites. To delete a folder or site, click to select it, then hit the delete key or select **Edit/Clear** from the menu.

To organize your bookmarks in Explorer, select **View/Explorer Bar** from the menu. Click the **Favorites** tab. Click the **Organize** button to create as many new folders or dividers as you need. (You can also select **Favorites/Organize Favorites/New Folder** and **Favorites/Organize/New Divider** from the menu.) Then drag the link icon of a site to move its link into a folder. You can drag and arrange folders and dividers to suit your needs. To change the name of a folder, click its name to highlight it, type in a new name, and press **Enter** (or **Return**). To delete a site, select it in a similar manner and press the **Delete** button. If the Explorer bar is open, you can also add the URL of a site you're currently visiting by clicking the **Add** button.

Access your bookmarks while on the road!

Visit Clickmarks.com (**http://www.clickmarks.com**). The service is free and includes online instructions for uploading your existing bookmarks. When you want to access them, log on to the site. Your links will appear in the browser window.

HOW TO PRINT AND SAVE WEB PAGES AND IMAGES

You can save and print Web pages and images, but you should only do so for your personal use. When Web site owners graciously publish their Web sites for all the world to enjoy, that doesn't mean you can take information from the site and use it however you please. If you want to use something for any other purpose than personal use, write the Web site owner and get permission. Anything else—including any type of distribution or adding an image or copied text to your own Web site—is a violation of copyright law. Don't do it! For more information, see **The Copyright Website** *(*http://www.benedict.com*) and the* **U.S.Copyright Office** *(*http://lcWeb.loc.gov/copyright*).*

• TO SAVE A WEB PAGE

After the page is fully loaded, select **File/Save As** from the menu. A dialog box will appear. Name the file and save it as either **text**, which you can open through a word processing program, or **source** which creates an HTML (the language that a Web page is written in) document you can read through your browser while offline.

A source document will include formatted text and place-ment holders for images, but it will not include the actual images unless you download each and place them in the same directory (or file) as you saved the source (HTML) document.

• TO PRINT A WEB PAGE

After the page has fully loaded, select **File/Print** from the menu. If the page has frames, first click in the frame you want to print (I often select some of the text to make sure the frame is selected). Then select **File/Print Frame** from the menu.

• TO SAVE AN IMAGE FROM A WEB PAGE TO YOUR HARD DRIVE

Position your mouse cursor over the image. Right-click on the image (click-hold on a Mac). A pop-up menu will appear. Select **Save Image As** or **Save Picture As**. You can later view it in your browser or in a graphics program.

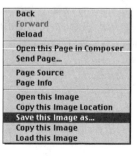

HOW TO SEND AND READ E-MAIL

Electronic mail, or e-mail, is one of the best forms of long distance communication and one of the most popular features of the Internet. Today's e-mail programs make reading and sending e-mail a snap. ·

If you are using American Online, simply click the **You Have Mail** icon on the Welcome screen to read or send e-mail. When sending e-mail to persons who have an AOL account, you can use the person's AOL address because everyone on AOL shares the suffix "@aol.com." If someone should ask for your e-mail address, remember to add the @aol.com suffix, otherwise it won't arrive. Whenever sending mail to persons not on AOL, you need to use the entire Internet address (with the proper suffix; e.g., **ctinfo@ctpub.com**), otherwise your letter will not arrive.

ISP users can use their browser's e-mail software. The vast majority of the time when your ISP or its software configures your browser to get you online, it also configures the mail preferences to allow you to send and retrieve e-mail. In Netscape Navigator, press Ctrl-2 to open Messenger—the mail program. On a Mac, click the Mail icon box in the lower-right hand corner of the browser's screen to open your in-box. Command-T retrieves new e-mail. In Internet Explorer, click the **Mail** icon in your Windows 95/98 tray to open the Outlook Express mail program (on a Mac, click the **Mail** icon in the Button Bar to open Outlook Express). ISP users can also use e-mail programs such as Eudora or Pegasus. If you want to use an e-mail program other than what came with your browser, contact your ISP's support center to help you configure it properly.

Want to see what's happening in other parts of the world? Visit **Earthcam** (**http://www.earthcam.com**)

GENERAL
WEB SAFETY TIPS

• Never give anyone your online password(s), credit card numbers, social security number, or mother's maiden name. Unfortunately, unscrupulous individuals can obtain your ISP username then e-mail you under the guise of being an AOL, Earthlink, or other ISP employee seeking to verify your account. Don't ever believe them, and do not respond. Instead, report such letters to your ISP.

• When selecting a password, don't use anything obvious—such as your date of birth. Instead, use your imagination, and create combinations of words and numbers. Periodically change your password.

• If a site requires you to create an identification name and password, make it different from your general username and password.

• Do not answer **any** type of junk mail, especially ones that say "respond to this letter to be removed from our list." Often a response indicates to the sender that it reached a valid user, and it may result in more junk mail. Never forward a chain letter or virus warning. Most are a hoax. Visit **Urban Legends Archive (http://www.urbanlegends.com)** and Vmyths (**http://www.Vmyths.com**) for information on chain letters and hoaxes. If you fear a genuine computer virus, check the **CERT Computer Virus Resource Center (http://www.cert.org/other_sources/viruses.html**) which includes extensive resources on computer viruses, including the latest virus-related news.

• Never click on hyperlinks within an e-mail message sent to you by a stranger. Such a site can whisk you to an official-looking Web site which claims one thing while the site is instead downloading a virus to your computer.

• Never open a file attachment from someone you don't know. It is the single best way to avoid contracting a computer virus.

WEB SHOPPING SAFETY TIPS

• Currently there are over 3,500 businesses on the Web that offer the **Better Business Bureau's BBBOnline** seal of approval (**http://www.bbbonline.com**). To obtain the seal, businesses must (among other things) provide security, friendly dispute resolution, and stand behind its advertised claims. If you see the seal on a site, click it. It should bring you to the BBB Online and provide details of the store. If you only see the seal or want to learn if a retail site is a participant, search the **BBB Online** (**http://www.bbbonline.org/database/search/default.cfm**).

• Read a site's privacy policy to understand what personal information will be requested and why and how it will be used. You can usually find a link to the site's privacy policy or by checking the site's legal terms. If you cannot find a privacy policy, e-mail the site and ask for it. If the site doesn't respond or doesn't have one, do business elsewhere.

• Some sites carry the TRUSTe seal. This seal is only awarded to sites that maintain established pri-

vacy principles. Clicking on the seal should bring you to the site's privacy policy. It should not bring you to the **TRUSTe** Web site (**http://www.truste.org**). If it does, be suspicious and search to see if the retail site is a participating member (**http://www.truste.org/users/users_lookup.html**).

• When considering a site to shop from, make sure you understand its return policies.

• Never give your credit card details within an e-mail message. E-mail is not secure.

• Never submit your credit card information or bank account information to an unsecured site. An unsecured site means the information in it can be intercepted.

- When shopping on the Web, always use a credit card. If you have any problem, you can contact the credit card company and either get the matter resolved or possibly get a refund. If for any reason, however, you are uncomfortable using a credit card, ask the site's customer support if an alternate form of payment can be made (check, money order, or COD).

- Always keep a written record of each Internet transaction, including the seller's name, address, telephone number; any e-mail messages; and a description of what you ordered, the price, and any terms. Be sure to compare it to the charge on your credit card bill.

RESOURCES FOR CONSUMER INFORMATION ON INTERNET PRIVACY ISSUES, SHOPPING, AND FRAUD

SAFE SHOPPING.ORG
http://www.safeshopping.org

This informational site from the American Bar Association will help you become a smarter online shopper. It offers well-organized content, detailing topics such as security, privacy, records, tips, and more.

INTERNET FRAUD COMPLAINT CENTER
http://www.ifccfbi.gov

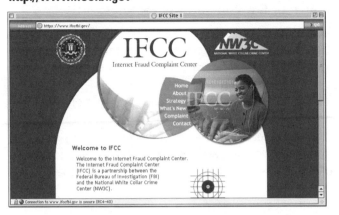

FTC KIDZ PRIVACY
http://www.ftc.gov/bcp/conline/edcams/kidzprivacy
This site sponsored by the Federal Trade Commission includes extensive resources and information to help you protect your children's privacy.

THE BETTER BUSINESS BUREAU
http://www.bbb.org

NATIONAL FRAUD INFORMATION CENTER
http://www.fraud.org

THE FEDERAL TRADE COMMISSION
http://www.ftc.gov
The Federal Trade Commission offers extensive articles and resources to insure your Web safety.

T I P

How To Tell If a Web Site is Secure and How to Turn on Your Browser Security Features

A secure Web site uses a form of sophisticated encryption that scrambles your transmitted information and keeps it safe from prying eyes. Your browser has features to alert you when you are entering and leaving a secure site and when you are sending information to an unencrypted site.

To open the security preferences in Netscape Navigator, click on the **padlock** icon in the lower left corner of the browser window. Select Navigator in the left column, check the **show warning** boxes, and click **OK**. To open the security preferences in Internet Explorer, select **Edit/Preferences** from the menu. Then select **Web Browser/Security** from the left column in the dialog box. Check the security alert boxes and click **OK**.

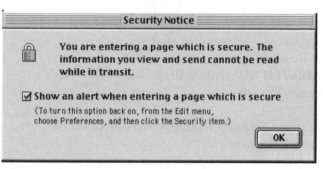

When entering a secure page, a dialog box will appear to alert you that the page is secure.

When at a secure site, you'll see an "s" after the <**http**> portion of the URL. An unsecured site will read <**http**>; a secure site will read <**https**>. For example: **https://www.buysafe.com/purchase**.

Additionally, on a secure site you will see an unbroken key or a closed padlock on the bottom of your browser window.

free Trip Planning from Large Travel Web Sites

The travel sites in this chapter are big—really big. In addition to including frequently changing articles and featured destinations, discussion forums, and travel resources, all allow you to book your entire vacation online. Keep in mind, however, that you do not have to book a thing. You can simply use these sites to stir ideas, to research and customize your itinerary, or to gather pricing information. Once it's time to make reservations, it's your choice whether to book your arrangements over the Web, use a travel agent, or a combination of both.

Note that most large travel agency sites require you to register before using their service, although some allow you to use their service once as a guest. Registration is free.

Tips for booking reservations:

- Check the customer support area of a site before doing business. Make sure you understand refund and cancellation policies, and if any fees are charged for changes, before you make your reservations.
- Keep multiple browser windows open to compare deals from different sites; they will vary.
- Check directly with a supplier to compare rates.
- If a deal sounds too good to be true, proceed with caution.
- Don't assume that just because it's on the Web, it's a bargain. Often a savvy travel agent can suggest alternate routes that can save you money.
- When considering a motel room, find out if you can see the room or obtain information as to where the hotel is located in the town you're visiting.
- Obtain written confirmation of any reservation you make.

🛒 *Web Sites of Large Online Travel Agencies*

THE QUILTROPOLIS TRAVEL DESK
http://www.Quiltropolis-Travel-Desk.com

This impressive travel portal is geared to traveling quilters. It offers hotel, flight, auto, golf, ski, tours, cruises, fishing, dining, theatre, news, and weather info and shopping. Best of all, you'll find a growing database of quilting trade show events and a wonderful selection of resources.

EXPEDIA
http://www.expedia.com

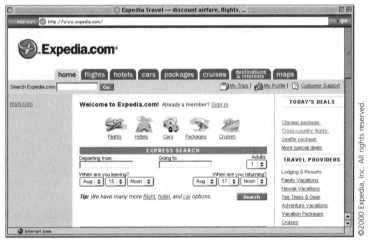

This full-service site is a one-stop resource for flights, rental cars, hotels, vacation packages, cruises, and more. When learning about places to visit, you can view 360 degree tours, watch slide shows, or take a two-minute virtual vacation. If you're on a budget, be sure to tap into Expedia's price matcher.

AMERICAN EXPRESS TRAVEL
http://travel.americanexpress.com

YAHOO TRAVEL
http://travel.yahoo.com

TRAVELOCITY
http://www.travelocity.com

Travelocity has joined with Preview Travel to offer fast bookings to airlines, rental cars, hotels, and thousands of vacation and cruise packages. It offers an e-mail fare notification service which monitors up to five flights and alerts you to any significant fare changes.

TRIP.COM
http://www.thetrip.com

ACCESSIBLE JOURNEYS
http://www.disabilitytravel.com

This company offers tours, cruises, rentals, companions and more for individuals with physical challenges.

AOL TRAVEL
http://www.aol.com/Webcenters/travel

BIZTRAVEL
http://www.biztravel.com

TRAVELSCAPE
http://www.travelscape

🛒 Web Sites for Last-Minute Travel Bargains and Travel Auction Sites

✋ Check the customer support area of a site before doing business. Make sure you understand refund and cancellation policies, and if any fees are charged for changes, before you make your reservations. Also see the Web Shopping Safety Tips in Chapter 1.

LASTMINUTETRAVEL.COM
http://www.lastminutetravel.com

1TRAVEL.COM
http://www.onetravel.com

1 STOP DISCOUNT TRAVEL
http://1stoptravel.com

AESU ONLINE
http://www.aesu.com

BUDGET TRAVEL
http://www.budgettravel.com

ECONOMY TRAVEL
http://www.economytravel.com

SKYAUCTION
http://www.Skyauction.com

PRICELINE.COM
http://www.priceline.com

✋ When using this site that "lets you name your own price," make sure you are ready to buy when naming your price. You need to supply your credit card number when completing a bid form. If Priceline finds a match to your criteria, it will immediately charge your credit card—and there are no returns.

Free Web Sites of Travel Magazines

Many Web sites of travel magazines offer extensive articles, active discussion forums where you can swap stories with fellow travelers, lodging and dining reviews, travel guides and tips, and plenty of helpful advice and resources. Here are some favorites:

ALL-ABROAD MAGAZINE
http://www.all-abroad.com

ARTHUR FROMMER'S BUDGET TRAVEL ONLINE
http://www.frommers.com

BETTER HOMES & GARDENS GUIDE TO TRAVEL
http://www.bhg.com/travel

CONDÉ NAST TRAVELER
http://www.cntraveler.com

FODOR'S
http://www.fodors.com

**JOURNEYWOMAN—
AN ONLINE MAGAZINE JUST FOR WOMEN**
http://www.journeywoman.com

LET'S GO
http://www.letsgo.com

LONELY PLANET ONLINE
http://www.lonelyplanet.com

NATIONAL GEOGRAPHIC TRAVELER
http://www.nationalgeographic.com/traveler

ROUGH GUIDES
http://www.roughguides.com

SHOESTRING TRAVEL
http://www.stratpub.com

**TOM PARSONS' BEST FARES
DISCOUNT TRAVEL MAGAZINE**
http://www.bestfares.com

free Tourism and Travel Guides

It was only a few years ago that obtaining travel guides meant either making a telephone call, sending a request by mail, or trekking off to the nearest travel agency. Today you need only to tap into the Web. The sites in this chapter will help you locate tourism information for almost any place in the world. If you still want full-color glossy brochures to page through while away from your computer, most sites offer them for free. You click on a button, fill out a form, and mouse-click your request. The brochures generally arrive in your mailbox within days.

To find information on a particular city visit **U.S.A. City Link** (**http://usacitylink.com**), which boasts the Internet's most comprehensive listing of cities. You select a state, and up pops a listing of cities. Select a city, and you'll find helpful links to sightseeing destinations, restaurants, entertainment, and more. **Online City Guide—Your Link to America** (**http://www.olcg.com**) is another excellent resource. It includes a vast selection of links to states, regions of the state, and over 1,700 cities. **Yahoo! Local** (**http://local.yahoo.com**) offers links to area guides, entertainment, travel and transportation, and more for each state in the country.

City Guides from CNN Travel (**http://www.cnn.com/TRAVEL/CITY.GUIDES**) includes lodging, restaurants, and a calendar of events for over 50 cities worldwide. You'll also find links to the latest travel news. **CitySearch** (**http://www.citysearch.com**) offers detailed information for a similar list of worldwide cities. **Digital City** (**http://www.digitalcity.com**) includes entertainment, sports, news, and more for larger cities in each state. **StateGuide.com** (**http://www.stateguide.com**) offers guides to over 4,000 communities in 50 states. **U.S.A. Online** (**http://www.usaol.com**) provides a state-by-state selection of businesses and related links, including traffic and transit info.

The Tourism Offices Worldwide Directory (**http://www.towd.com**) offers links to official government tourism offices, convention and visitors bureaus, chambers of commerce, and similar agencies that provide unbiased travel information for countries around the world and U.S. states.

To find the official Web page of each U.S. state (for general state information), type <**http://www.state.XX.us**>, except insert the two-letter state abbreviation in place of the XX. For example, for Nevada, it's **http://www.state.nv.us**; for California it's **http://www.state.ca.us**. For additional state information, see 50States.com (**http://www.50states.com**).

No need to ever visit a travel agent again for travel brochures. Instead, tap into **Desteo—The World's Most Complete Resource for Free Travel Information** (**http://www.desteo.com**). This site is amazing. It offers over 15,000 free travel guides, maps, and brochures. You can search by region, location, or a particular activity. You click on the items you want added to your cart, then you check out. It's all free. You don't even pay for postage!

FREE
STATE TOURISM GUIDES

ALABAMA
http://www.touralabama.org

ALASKA
http://www.travelalaska.com

ARIZONA
http://www.arizonaguide.com

ARKANSAS
http://www.1800natural.com

CALIFORNIA
http://gocalif.ca.gov/index

COLORADO
http://www.colorado.com

CONNECTICUT
http://www.tourism.state.ct.us

DELAWARE
http://www.state.de.us/tourism.
htm

FLORIDA
http://www.flausa.com

GEORGIA
http://www.georgia.org

HAWAII
http://www.gohawaii.com

IDAHO
http://www.visitid.org

ILLINOIS
http://www.enjoyillinois.com

INDIANA
http://www.enjoyindiana.com

IOWA
http://www.traveliowa.com

KANSAS
http://www.kansascommerce.com

KENTUCKY
http://www.kytourism.com

LOUISIANA
http://www.louisianatravel.com

MAINE
http://www.visitmaine.com

MARYLAND
http://www.mdisfun.org

MASSACHUSETTS
http://www.mass-vacation.com

MICHIGAN
http://www.michigan.org

MINNESOTA
http://www.exploreminnesota
.com

MISSISSIPPI
http://www.visitmississippi.org

MISSOURI
http://www.missouritourism.com

MONTANA
http://www.visitmt.com

NEBRASKA
http://www.visitnebraska.org

NEVADA
http://www.travelnevada.com

NEW HAMPSHIRE
http://www.visitnh.gov

NEW JERSEY
http://www.state.nj.us/travel

NEW MEXICO
http://www.newmexico.org

NEW YORK
http://www.iloveny.state.ny.us

NORTH CAROLINA
http://www.visitnc.com

NORTH DAKOTA
http://discovernd.com/visiting

OHIO
http://www.ohiotourism.com

OKLAHOMA
http://www.travelok.com

OREGON
http://www.traveloregon.com

PENNSYLVANIA
http://www.experiencepa.com

SOUTH CAROLINA
http://www.travelsc.com

SOUTH DAKOTA
http://www.travelsd.com

TENNESSEE
http://www.state.tn.us/vacat.html

TEXAS
http://www.traveltex.com

UTAH
http://www.utah.com

VERMONT
http://www.travel-vermont.com

VIRGINIA
http://www.virginia.org

WASHINGTON
http://www.tourism.wa.gov

WEST VIRGINIA
http://www.wvWeb.com

WISCONSIN
http://www.tourism.state.wi.us

WYOMING
http://wyomingtourism.org

DISTRICT OF COLUMBIA
http://www.washington.org

Thinking of vacationing in the Caribbean?
First visit The Caribbean (**http://www.caribtourism.com**). Sponsored by the Caribbean Tourism Organization, this site includes information, such as a calendar of events and weather, on its 32 member countries. While at the site, you can order a free Caribbean vacation planner.

free Help for International Travelers

You can bring home fabric from another country, but can you bring home a plant? Do certain countries present any health concerns you should be aware of? Can you drink the water? How much is the U.S. dollar worth? How long will it take to get a passport? Avoid last-minute surprises by tapping into the sites in this chapter before leaving home.

U.S. STATE DEPARTMENT— BUREAU OF CONSULAR AFFAIRS
http://travel.state.gov

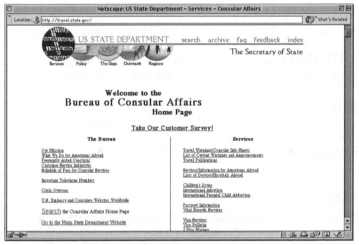

Tap into this site to learn about worldwide embassies and consulates, passport information, and guidance for American citizens abroad.
Travel Warnings & Consular Sheets and Public Information
*(***http://travel.state.gov/travel_warnings.html***) includes a list of countries each with a description, entry requirements, crime information, criminal penalties, medical facilities, medical and other health information, traffic safety and road conditions, aviation safety, children's information, and consulate information.*

TIP

Want to Learn a Foreign Language?

Travlang (**http://www.travlang.com**), created by Michael C. Martin, teaches basic words, numbers, and other phrases for shopping, dining, directions, etc. in the language you select. Sound files and myriad resources are included. Also try **International Language Development** (**http://www.ild.com**) which offers free French, German, Japanese, Korean, Russian, and Spanish online language lessons, all with sound files.

CENTERS FOR DISEASE CONTROL AND PREVENTION
http://www.cdc.gov/travel/index.htm
Comprehensive information on vaccinations, safe food and water, and tips for traveling with children.

HER OWN WAY—
ADVICE FOR THE WOMAN TRAVELER
http://www.dfait-maeci.gc.ca/travel/consular/16009-e.htm
Published by the Department of Foreign Affairs and International Trade, read topics such as lessening culture shock, networking, avoiding harassment, coping with foreign bathrooms, and more.

TRAVELERS' TIPS ON BRINGING FOOD, PLANT, AND ANIMAL PRODUCTS INTO THE UNITED STATES
http://www.aphis.usda.gov/oa/travel.html

TRAVELERS MEDICAL AND VACCINATION CENTRE
http://www.tmvc.com.au
This Australian group is one of the top travel medical providers in the world.

THE UNIVERSAL CURRENCY CONVERTER
http://www.xe.net/ucc
No bells and whistles, just a straightforward online converter to perform a foreign rate exchange.

TRAVEL HEALTH ONLINE
http://www.tripprep.com

Travel Health ONLINE

Welcome
world travelers. We salute your spirit! Shoreland, the trusted resource of travel medicine practitioners around the globe, created Travel Health Online to help you on your way to a safe, healthy adventure.

DESTINATION INFORMATION
Afghanistan ... Zimbabwe

TRAVELER INFORMATION
Altitude Illness ... Yellow Fever

TRAVEL MEDICINE PROVIDERS
Across the USA & Around the World

Version 4.0 or later of Microsoft or Netscape browser is **recommended**.
See *Tips for Browsing* .

© 2000 Shoreland, Inc.

Select a country and learn its general information, health risks, and health precautions. Read pre-departure preparations and post-trip considerations. A list of travel medical providers is available, as is other helpful information such as emergency planning, jet lag, avoiding crime, protection from insects, and motion sickness precautions.

🛒 INTERNATIONAL HEALTH INSURANCE FROM WALKABOUT TRAVEL GEAR
http://www.walkabouttravelgear.com/insure.htm
This informative article details resources offering international health insurance and explains why you may need it.

INTERNATIONAL TRAVEL TIP BAZAAR FROM JOURNEYWOMAN
http://www.journeywoman.com/friendlytips/friendly.html
A large collection of insightful reader tips, such as why Agnes of Toronto always travels with a small flashlight and Darcy from Vancouver put electrical tape over the fancy name of her camera.

🛒 CORPORATE TRAVEL SAFETY
http://www.corporatetravelsafety.com
Travel Safety Tips *includes over 110 pages of tips useful to any traveler.*

THE WORLDWIDE HOLIDAY AND FESTIVAL SITE
http://www.holidayfestival.com
If you're planning on shopping while traveling, make sure you're not arriving when all the stores are closed due to a holiday.

CURRENCY CONVERTER FROM OANDA.COM—
THE CURRENCY SITE
http://www.oanda.com
http://www.oanda.com/convert/classic
Not only can you learn the going rate of a McDonalds's Big Mac in countries around the world, but you can convert over 164 currencies instantly. Print out a wallet-size currency cheat sheet to help you convert money while on the road.

 INTERNATIONAL DRIVER'S LICENSE
http://www.idl-international.com
If you're planning on driving while abroad, consider obtaining an International driver's license. You must be a valid U.S. driver to obtain one, and the International license is only acceptable when accompanied by valid U.S. driver's license.

MOTO EUROPA—
A GUIDE TO EUROPEAN MOTOR TRAVEL
http://www.ideamerge.com/motoeuropa
If you're thinking about driving in Europe, visit this super site founded by Eric Bredesen of Iowa. Online Guide includes a wealth of articles dealing with logistics, borders, fuel, road signs and signals, on-the-other-side parking, telephone codes, ferries, and more. You'll also find a country-by-country list detailing what you need to know while driving through it, such as license requirements, general driving info, photos of road signs, accident and emergency situations, and translations.

TIP

Does anybody really know what time it is? **Local Times Around the World** (**http://times.clari.net.au**) provides the local time and other information for the country or island of your choice.

free Guides to Parks, Beaches, and Other Family Travel Fun

Festivals. Picnics. Drive-in movies. And my most vivid memories of family fun: summer excursions to the Jersey shore—the sun-splashed days playing on the beach, building sandcastles, jumping ocean waves—the long strolls up and down the boardwalk, riding carousels and rollercoasters, eating French fries and funnel cakes, and spending quarters on games of chance. The sites in this chapter offer guidance and ideas for creating a bright patchwork of fun for you and your loved ones. For fair and festival information, see Chapter 10.

Free Help for Traveling with Youngsters

FAMILY TRAVEL FORUM
http://www.familytravelforum.com
Their motto? Have kids, still travel.

TINY TRAVELERS
http://www.tinytravelers.net
Traveling with a difficult child? Wondering whether you should take the kids or leave them at home? These are some of the issues discussed at this site dedicated to the safe, fun, and pleasurable travel with children. Related links are included.

BETTER HOMES & GARDENS TRAVEL
http://www.bhg.com/travel/
Visit the kids' travel page for lots of ideas on keeping the little ones happy during transit.

TRAVEL WITH KIDS FROM ABOUT.COM
http://travelwithkids.about.com
Teresa Plowright offers terrific articles and heaps of links—all related to traveling with kids. Learn which major hotel chains are kid-friendly and why it may make sense to rent strollers at your destination. Find out about specialized family tours, and get oodles of family vacation ideas. There's also a free e-mail newsletter you can subscribe to.

Free Directories to Beaches and National Parks

BEST BEACHES IN THE USA
http://www.petrix.com/beaches

ALL BEACHES
http://www.allbeaches.net

GREAT OUTDOOR RECREATION PAGES
http://www.gorp.com

NATIONAL PARK SERVICE TRAILS
www.nps.gov/trails

THE NATIONAL PARK SERVICE—PARK NET
http://www.nps.gov

This informative, colorful site offers a searchable database of national parks.

GRAND CANYON NATIONAL PARK
http://www.thecanyon.com/nps

GRAND CANYON EXPLORER
http://www.crl.com/~ddickson/parks.html

Free Guides to Amusement Parks, Theme Parks, and Other Family Fun

AMERICA'S BEST ONLINE
http://www.americasbestonline.com
Favorites include:

• THE TOP 10 ZOOS AND AQUARIUMS
http://www.americasbestonline.com/zoo.htm
Where you'll also find a large link directory to other zoos around the country.

• U.S.A.'S TOP ROLLERCOASTERS BY KEVIN HULME
http://www.americasbestonline.com/roller.htm

• U.S.A.'S BEST CAROUSELS
http://www.americasbestonline.com/merry.htm

THEME PARKS AT ABOUT.COM
http://themeparks.about.com
Robert Brown is your guide to theme parks. Related sites such as zoos, marine life parks, carnivals, and the circus, are included.

If you're going to take a long drive, why not make it a scenic one?

Search **National Scenic Byways** (**http://www.byways.org**), sponsored by the Federal Highway Administration, for scenic byways throughout the U.S. You can also view photos, read news items, and request a free map.

TIM MELAGO'S DIRECTORY OF AMUSEMENT PARK AND ROLLERCOASTER LINKS
http://users.sgi.net/~rollocst/amuse.html

FUN GUIDE
http://www.funguide.com

AMUSEMENT LINKS ONE SOURCE
http://members.aol.com/parklinks/links.htm

DRIVE-IN THEATERS
http://www.driveintheater.com

WORLD'S LARGEST ROADSIDE ATTRACTIONS
http://www.infomagic.net/~martince/index.htm
Kitsch reigns, where if it's proclaimed the world's largest—such as the largest catsup bottle or the biggest strawberry—you'll find it here.

🛒 OFFICIAL DISNEY.COM
http://disney.go.com/DisneyWorld/index2.html
The official site to all things Disney.

WERNER'S UNOFFICIAL GUIDE TO DISNEY WORLD
http://www.disneyfan.com

SIX FLAG THEME PARKS
http://www.sixflags.com
Learn about the 28 Six Flag theme parks located around the country.

ROADSIDE AMERICA
http://www.roadsideamerica.com
Peruse more than 700 pages of offbeat tourist attractions.

CHAPTER 6

free Directories to Hotels and Other Lodging

My good friend Cathy prefers a five-star hotel with porters, room service, and a luscious chocolate mint left on her pillow each evening after the bed is turned down. Janet prefers the quaint ambience and excellent food that a bed & breakfast offers. MaryAnn looks for a room at her favorite hotel chain. Whatever your needs, the directories in this chapter will help locate your lodging ideal. For those who like to rough it, campgrounds are included.

Before making a hotel reservation, be sure you understand refund and cancellation policies, and if any fees are charged for changes, before you make your reservations. Also see the Web Shopping Safety Tips in Chapter 1.

FREE DIRECTORIES TO U.S. HOTELS AND RESORTS

U.S.A. HOTEL GUIDE.COM
http://www.usahotelguide.com
An extensive directory of over 40,000 hotels, resorts and inns throughout the U.S.A.

HISTORIC HOTELS OF AMERICA— NATIONAL TRUST FOR HISTORIC PRESERVATION
http://www.nthp.org/main/hotels
A diverse collection of 145 hotels that have faithfully maintained their historic architecture.

INTERNET LODGING DIRECTORY SEARCH
http://www.usa-lodging.com

HOTELS ONLINE
http://www.hotelsonline.com

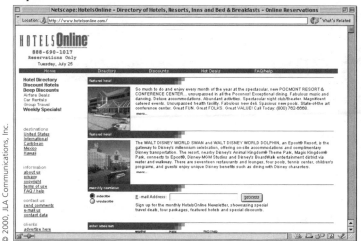

This extensive site boasts the largest directory of U.S. hotels, resorts, and inns. Photos, information, surrounding area attractions, directions, and more are included.

Free Directories to International Hotels and Resorts

RESORTS AND LODGES.COM
http://www.ResortsandLodges.com
This searchable directory contains over 8,000 resorts, also organized by location, type of resort, and activity (such as beach, shopping, or sightseeing). A section on family resorts is included.

RESORTS ONLINE
http://www.resortsonline.com
Search for resorts worldwide by selecting an activity (such as safari, spa, riding, marina, casino, scuba, castle) or entering keywords such as activities, amenities, or locations.

HOTEL GUIDE—
THE INTERNATIONAL HOTEL DIRECTORY
http://www.hotelguide.com

Hotel Guide includes a searchable directory to over 60,000 hotels in more than 200 countries. The location of many hotels throughout North American and Europe can be displayed on a map, together with nearby points of interest.

ALL-HOTELS.COM
http://www.all-hotels.com

Richard Irwin and Nick Eckert of Scotland created All-Hotels.com, a gateway to over 60,000 bookable hotels and B&Bs worldwide. When visiting the site, click onto All-Abroad to read a free, fascinating online travel magazine.

Free Directories of Bed & Breakfast Inns

"A wonderful alternative to a chain hotel is a bed and break-fast, and they are often priced more reasonably than you'd think. You'll meet interesting people, have a much better breakfast than hotel cereal, and maybe even get a soak in a Jacuzzi."
—Rob and Lynn Holland (**http://www.planetpatchwork.com**)

CANADIAN BED & BREAKFAST ONLINE
http://www.bbcanada.com

GUIDE TO HISTORIC BED & BREAKFAST INNS
http://www.enteract.com/~scndempr

PAMELA LANIER'S BED & BREAKFAST GUIDE
http://www.travelguides.com/bandb

BED & BREAKFAST INNS ONLINE
http://www.bbonline.com

A one-stop guide to locating and making reservations at over 2,750 B&B inns worldwide, including inns that offer distinctive features, such as being located in the mountains; near a shore, ocean, or lake; that have overnight facilities for horses; or that are on the National Register of Historic Places. This site also features a huge collection of over 1,000 yummy inn-tested recipes, with new recipes added weekly.

INN SITE—THE INTERNET DIRECTORY
OF BED & BREAKFASTS
http://www.innsite.com

Browse numerous pages of B&B information by selecting a U.S. state, or by doing a keyword search. You'll find photos, detailed descriptions, amenities, local sightseeing, and more.

Free Directories to Campgrounds

KOA (KAMPGROUNDS OF AMERICA) KAMPGROUNDS
http://www.koakampgrounds.com

CAMP USA
http://www.campusa.com

GO CAMPING AMERICA
http://www.gocampingamerica.com/main.html

THE INTERNET CAMPING DIRECTORY
http://www.rvpark.com

CHAPTER 7

free Transportation Guides and Help

When I was a kid, my family always traveled by car. We all loaded into my dad's Pontiac and ventured off on a meandering journey filled with multiple stops and detours. It wasn't until I was older that I learned the joy of flying. There's something magical about leaving the deep freeze of a New Jersey winter and arriving in the warm, sunny climate of southern California hours later. Some say it's not the destination, but the journey that matters. I say when it's vacation time, different factors affect which matters more. In either case, transportation is key.

Free Airport Guides, Tips, and Help

LEARN2 SHOP FOR BARGAIN AIRFARES
http://www.learn2.com
http://www.learn2.com/09/0904/0904.asp
Want to save some money on airfares? This unbiased tutorial from Learn2.com explains how you can become a savvy consumer.

LOWEST AIRFARE TIPS
http://www.traveldiscounters.com/tips.html

QUICKAID AIRPORT DIRECTORY
http://www.quickaid.com
For each airport listed you'll find links to related ground transportation, hotel info, airline companies, a terminal map, and Yellow Pages.

AIRLINE TOLL-FREE NUMBERS
http://www.princeton.edu/Main/air800.html
Princeton University offers a comprehensive list of airlines, their toll-free numbers, and links to their Web sites.

AVIATION CONSUMER PROTECTION DIVISION
http://www.dot.gov/airconsumer

🛒 RULES OF THE AIR FROM ONE TRAVEL
http://www.onetravel.com
http://www.onetravel.com/rules/rules.cfm
Terry Trippler, an authority on airline carriage rules, shares her knowledge and answers common airline concerns.

AIRSAFE.COM—USEFUL INFORMATION FOR THE TRAVELING PUBLIC
http://www.airsafe.com
You'll find extensive articles and links to passenger advice, travel tips, answers to common airline travel questions, and much more.

FLIGHT PROGRESS.COM
http://www.flightprogress.com
Monitor the progress of specific airline flights within the United States and Canada.

LOOKING FOR GOOD RESTAURANTS WHILE IN TRANSIT?

Sure, you can stop and eat at fast-food restaurants along the Interstate exits. But you don't have to. Visit these sites before leaving on your trip to find some good alternatives:

• DINER CITY
http://www.dinercity.com
An online guide to American classic diners.

• DINENET—MENUS ONLINE
http://www.dinenet.com

• FIND DINING
http://www.zagat.com
Includes restaurant reviews for over 20,000 cities.

• PUB CRAWLER
http://www.pubcrawler.com

• CHOWHOUND
http://www.chowhound.com/main.html
Jim Leff, a restaurant reviewer for Bloomberg News Radio (WBBR-AM) and author, offers articles guaranteed to make you hungry.

🛒 Web Sites Specializing in Discount Airfare

Discounted fares are also offered through many large travel sites. See Chapter 2 for more details.

> ✋ *Check the customer support area of a site before doing business. Make sure you understand refund and cancellation policies, and if any fees are charged for changes, before you make your reservations.*

- **WEB FLYER**
http://www.Webflyer.com

- **AIRLINE TICKETS WHOLESALE**
http://www.traveldiscounters.com

- **AIRLINES OF THE WEB**
http://flyaow.com

- **SKY AUCTION**
http://www.skyauction.com

- **CHEAP TICKETS**
http://www.cheaptickets.com

- **AIRFARE.COM**
http://www.airfare.com

- **4AIRLINES**
http://www.4airlines.com

- **AIR COURIER ASSOCIATION**
http://www.aircourier.org

🛅 Free Rail, Bus, and Subway Travel Guides

- **TRAIN TRAVEL AT ABOUT.COM**
http://traintravel.about.com

- **AMTRAK**
http://www.amtrak.com

- **NORTH AMERICAN RAILROAD TERMINAL**
http://www.railterminal.com/touridx.shtml

- **METROPOLITAN TRANSPORTATION AUTHORITY**
http://www.mta.nyc.ny.us

GREYHOUND LINES
http://www.greyhound.com

RAIL EUROPE
http://www.raileurope.com

THE SUBWAY NAVIGATOR
http://www.subwaynavigator.com/bin/cities/english

VIA RAIL CANADA
http://www.viarail.ca/en.index.html

UK RAILWAYS ON THE NET
http://www.rail.co.uk

LINKS TO RAILWAYS
http://www.sentex.net/~kramer/ici/Railways.html

SUBWAYS OF THE WORLD
http://www.reed.edu/%7Ereyn/transport.html
Robert Reynolds provides links to world subway and other transportation information resources.

Free Automotive Help and Guides to Rental Cars

AUTO REPAIRS AND MAINTENANCE FROM AUTOSITE.COM
http://www.autosite.com/garage/garmenu.asp
Before driving on your next vacation, check the handy articles on this site for car maintenance and general repair info.

AAA
http://www.aaa.com
Learn about AAA membership benefits.

CAR RENTAL LINKS FROM BEST FARES
http://www.bestfares.com/cyberlinks/car.htm
A comprehensive resource to car rental links, including unusual car rentals such as campers and Rent A Wreck.

WOMAN MOTORIST
http://www.womanmotorist.com
Women and men both will appreciate the well-written, extensive articles covering everything from car reviews and travel to car maintenance and safety in this free online Internet magazine.

Free Guides to Popular Rental Car Companies

- **ALAMO CAR RENTAL**
http://www.goalamo.com

- **AVIS RENT A CAR**
http://www.avis.com

- **BUDGET RENT A CAR**
http://www.budgetrentacar.com

- **DOLLAR RENT A CAR**
http://www.dollar.com

- **ENTERPRISE RENT A CAR**
http://www.enterprise.com

- **THE HERTZ CORPORATION**
http://www.hertz.com

- **NATIONAL CAR RENTAL**
http://www.nationalcar.com

- **THRIFTY CAR RENTAL**
http://www.thrifty.com

- **RAINBOW WHEELS**
http://www.bestfares.com/cyberlinks/car.htm
Wheelchair accessible rental vans serving Michigan, Indiana, Ohio, and Florida.

TRAFFIC STATION.COM
http://www.trafficstation.com
Check real-time traffic reports in 28 major cities (including Houston) and avoid gridlock and other nasty road conditions. Reports can be sent to your pager, cell phone, Web phone, or PDA.

free Guides to Maps, Directions, and Weather Reports

Some people have a natural gift of direction—a built-in compass allowing them to drive exactly where they want to go. Others will drive for miles in unfamiliar territory before pulling into a gas station and sheepishly asking an attendant for directions. Regardless of where you fall on the driving-direction scale, cruise over to an online map site for free printable directions before starting your journey. Sites such as **MapQuest** (**http://www.mapquest.com**) work in a similar manner: You type in your starting location and destination. Then, with the click of a mouse, maps and driving instructions are formulated. Directions include every step of the way with information such as street names, turns and exits, mileage, and approximate travel time. You can zoom in or out on displayed maps, printing what you need. Some sites also offer the ability to find businesses—hotels, restaurants, and even quilt stores—in a particular radius from a city and state. Because no matter where you're going you will want to know the weather conditions, sites offering weather reports are included.

Tips for using online map sites:

• If you're not familiar with the area you will be traveling to, gather directions from a couple of sites to compare consistency.

• Obtain separate directions for various points along your route.

• Use the zoom-in feature to print maps with streets names in case you need to plan an alternate route.

• Remember that sites estimating travel time do not take into consideration traffic jams or detours.

Sites Offering Free Maps and Directions

MAPQUEST
http://www.mapquest.com

This is one of the most comprehensive map sites on the Web. It can quickly generate maps for practically any place you want to go and produce driving directions for destinations in the U.S., Canada, Mexico, and Europe—highlighting restaurants and attractions, if desired. MapQuest includes other perks such as message boards, Yellow and White Pages, live traffic updates, movie listings, weather, maps of airports and national parks, city guides, and information on finding top-rated restaurants and hotels.

ZIP2.COM
http://www.zip2.com

In addition to obtaining maps and directions, you can locate various businesses near a specific address. Did someone say quilt store?

MAPS AT EXPEDIA.COM
http://www.expediamaps.com

RAND McNALLY
http://www.randmcnally.com

🛒 MAPS.COM
http://www.maps.com

Although there are a few more clicks needed to produce maps and directions, I found the directions to be some of the cleanest. You can include an intermediate destination and select among different options such as a route with major highways or no major highways. You can also search for listings such as theaters, airports, arenas, stadiums, hospitals, and shopping centers within a specified distance from an address.

🛒 GTE SUPERPAGES.COM
http://www.superpages.com

Although maps are generated by MapQuest, there are options for door-to-door or city-to-city directions. If you're not familiar with the exact name of the place you're driving to, you can select a category to help you.

🎒 Free Guides to Weather Reports

THE WEATHER CHANNEL
http://www.weather.com

Type in a city or zip code and instant weather conditions and a 7-day forecast appears.

USA TODAY WEATHER
http://www.usatoday.com/weather

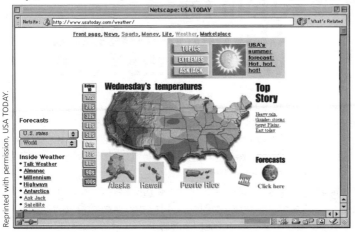

Learn the current weather happenings throughout the U.S., including forecasts for regions around the world. Weather-related stories and resources are included.

CNN WEATHER
http://www.cnn.com/WEATHER

ACCUWEATHER.COM
http://www.accuweather.com

NATIONAL WEATHER SERVICE
http://www.nws.noaa.gov

THE WEATHER UNDERGROUND
http://www.wunderground.com

TROPICAL STORM WATCH
http://www.fema.gov/fema/trop.htm

CHAPTER 9

free Help for Staying Connected While on the Road

No matter where your travels take you, the Web makes it easier than ever to stay connected with family and friends. E-mail is far less expensive than long-distance telephone calls, and it's something you can send and read at your leisure. Don't have a laptop? No problem. Most libraries, hotels, business centers, and colleges offer Internet access. Many airports have pay-per-minute Web terminals. Even Kampgrounds of America is encouraging the installation of computer kiosks. Internet (or "cyber") cafés are springing up everywhere. And if you're visiting friends, chances are they have an online connection you can tap into.

TECHNOTRAVEL
http://pobox.com/~technotravel

© 2000 Anders Andersen

Replete with guidance and resources, this site details how to access the Net—with or without a computer—while traveling.

STEVE KROPLA'S WORLD WIDE PHONE GUIDE
http://www.kropla.com/phones.htm

Steve details line testers, phone plugs and adapters, dial tones, in-line connectors, and practically everything else you need to know about hooking up your modem just about anywhere in the world. He includes an extensive list of resources in case there is any equipment you need to buy.

ROADNEWS.COM
http://www.roadnews.com

Enlightening articles for persons traveling with a laptop computer. Have a question? Join the discussion group for answers to your road-traveling woes.

AT&T WORLDWIDE TRAVELER
http://www.att.com/traveler/flyby_d.html

Contains access codes for AT&T international calling services worldwide.

🛒 ROAD WARRIOR—
GEAR FOR THE MOBILE PROFESSIONAL
http://www.warrior.com/index.html

🛒 TRAVELER'S FORUM FROM LAPTOP TRAVEL
http://www.laptoptravel.com/forum/default.asp
Fellow travelers share unique solutions for traveling with laptop computers. Topics include modems, international access, hotel room connections, RV/mobile computing products, wired campgrounds, wireless solutions, and more.

🏠 Free Directories of Internet or "Cyber" Cafés

Cyber cafés are a great place to meet local residents and fellow travelers. However, some cafés seem to vanish in the night. Rather than assuming a particular café will be open when you arrive, make a telephone call or send an e-mail and confirm the café is still open for business.

CYBERCAFES.COM
http://www.netcafes.com
The database of cafés is constantly being updated. Last count? Over 3,600 cafés in 138 countries!

INTERNET CAFÉS IN THE USA
http://www.netcafeguide.com/USA.htm

CURIOUS CAT CYBER CAFÉ CONNECTIONS
http://www.curiouscat.com/travel/cybercafe.htm

CYBER CAFÉ SEARCH ENGINE
http://cybercaptive.com

TIP

Need to receive or send a fax?
Try a Web-based fax service, such as **eFax.com**
(**http://www.efax.com**), Fax PC (**http://www.faxpc.com**),
and EasyFax (**http://easyfax.net**).

Accessing Your E-mail While Away from Home

Find a computer with Internet access, and chances are you can tap into your e-mail. These sites will show you the way.

AOL MAIL
http://www.aolmail.aol.com
Read, delete, and send AOL mail from the Web.

MAILSTARTPLUS
http://www.mailstartplus.com
This free services allows you to access e-mail from up to five POP3 e-mail accounts through the Web.

USING E-MAIL WHILE ON THE ROAD
http://www.emailaddresses.com/guide_road.htm
This article from EmailAddresses.com explains what you need to know and includes myriad resources and links.

Sites Offering Free E-Mail

Using a Web-based free e-mail account is a great deal, especially when on the road. They are easy to set up and access. For a large directory of free e-mail services, articles about free e-mail, and many related resources, tap into **Free EMail Address Directory** (**http://www.emailaddresses.com**). Here are some popular free e-mail services.

• **ALTAVISTA E-MAIL**
http://altavista.iname.com

• **MAIL CITY**
http://www.mailcity.com

• **E-MAIL.COM**
http://www.email.com

• **NET ADDRESS**
http://www.netaddress.usa.net

• **EXCITE MAIL**
http://www.mailexcite.com

• **YAHOO MAIL**
http://mail.yahoo.com

TIPS FOR TRAVELING WITH A LAPTOP COMPUTER

• Before leaving home, check with your ISP for a local number at your destination. If you're an AOL user, type Keyword: **Access**. Then do a search to find a number in your desired location.

• If no local number is available, determine whether a toll-free 800 number is available. Although you will pay about $6 per hour to use the number, it's probably a bargain compared to dialing long distance. AOL's 800 access number is 1-800-716-0023 and can be used anywhere in the U.S., Puerto Rico, and the U.S. Virgin Islands. A surcharge of $6 per hour will be added to your monthly bill.

• Don't check your laptop computer with your luggage. Carry it on.

• To help prevent having your laptop computer stolen while going through a metal detector at an airport, avoid long lines. If possible, wait until the person ahead of you walks through the detector before putting your computer on the conveyor belt.

• Find out if the hotel you are staying at uses a digital phone system. If so, don't use it. Best-case scenario is a "no dial tone" message; worst-case scenario is your modem will fry. Instead, ask if an analog data port is available. If not, visit sites such as **Road Warrior** (**http://www.warrior.com**) or **Laptop Travel** (**http://www.laptoptravel.com**) to purchase a digital-to-analog converter.

• Some hotel phone systems don't use a dial-tone sound, or it's weak or unusual sounding. If your modem fails to detect a dial tone, head over to your modem control panel and check the "ignore dial tone" box.

- Many hotels require that you dial a number, such as 9, to get an outside line. If so, you need to add that number and a comma in front of your phone-number string in the appropriate control panel. Inserting a comma creates a delay before your modem dials the next number. It generally creates a long enough pause to allow a connection to an outside line. If the pause is not long enough, add a second comma to the number string.

- Take a long (12-foot) phone cord with you in case the wall phone-jack is in an odd location.

- To avoid a wall phone-jack altogether, bring along an adapter that allows you to connect two phone cords together. This way you can connect the cord that goes to the phone with the cord that goes to the modem.

- Be sure you have an appropriate adapter with you in case you need to convert a three-pronged plug to a two-pronged plug.

- Bring along an extension cord. You never know where the electrical outlet will be.

- If traveling out of the country, visit **Steve Kropla's International Travel Page** (**http://www.kropla.com**) for telephone and electrical outlet information.

TIP

Looking to buy a notebook computer?

Visit **Notebook Review** (**http://www.notebookreview.com**) for buyer's guides, tips, a message board, and related articles. At **C/Net** (**http://www.cnet.com**) look under *Hardware Reviews, Notebooks*, to read reviews and recommendations.

free Guides to Festivals, Fairs, Art and Craft, Sewing, and Needlework Shows

Summer isn't summer without attending at least one festival. Sure, you're cavorting around in 100 degree weather, but lords and ladies are recreating medieval times. Wine and cheese extravaganzas await you. Artisans are eager to sell their wares. And let's not forget the more refined—ahem—festivals featuring watermelon seed-spitting contests, tug-of-war battles in the mud, and greasy, messy foods to eat. No matter what the festival, the Web will help you find the latest goings-on in your home state or around the world.

Start your search by visiting **Festivals.com—Celebrating the World of Festivals and Events (http://www.festivals.com)**. This whopper site includes over 33,000 events in its database. Search by date, region, or keyword or peruse sections such as arts, culture, or music. This site often includes more events in my home state than I find in local newspapers.

Free Guides to Festivals and Events

WORLD WIDE EVENTS
http://wwevents.com
This is a great site to find out what's going on in your backyard or places far from home.

WHATSGOINGON.COM
http://www.whatsgoingon.com
A fun site offering juicy opinions on what's going on where. Be sure to check out the Top 10 lists.

RENAISSANCE FAIRE
http://www.renaissance-faire.com

Patrick Bock created and maintains this resource to all things related to the Renaissance Faire (known as "Renfaire" to insiders), including a directory of every fair and festival in each state of the country.

FESTPASS.COM
http://www.festpass.com
A searchable database to over 1,300 European festivals.

FESTIVAL FINDER
http://www.festivalfinder.com
If you're looking for a music festival, this is the place to visit. It covers the latest details on over 1,500 music festivals in North America—everything from alternative and classical to reggae and rock. Select your favorite type of music or search by date, location, performers, or festival name.

SOUTHERN FESTIVALS
http://southfest.com
Information on festivals, fairs, and events held in Alabama, Georgia, North Carolina, South Carolina, Virginia, and Florida.

Free Guides to Arts, Crafts, Needlework, and Sewing Festivals and Expos

No pie-throwing contests here, but you will find many not-to-be-missed shows featuring arts, crafts, sewing, and needlework.

SHOW GUIDE FROM NETCRAFTS ONLINE GALLERY AND MAGAZINE
http://www.netcrafts.com/shows/shows.html
State-by-state guide of art, crafts, antiques, and other fairs and festivals.

CRAFTS AMERICA SHOWS
http://www.craftsamericashows.com

KUTZTOWN PENNSYLVANIA GERMAN FESTIVAL
http://www.kutztownfestival.com

PHILADELPHIA MUSEUM OF ART CRAFT SHOW
http://www.libertynet.org/pmacraft/index.html

COUNTRY CRAFT HOME AND GIFT SHOWS
http://www.country-craft.com

CREATIVE SEWING AND NEEDLEWORK FESTIVAL— CANADA
http://www.csnf.com

Culture Finder (**http://www.culturefinder.com**) offers a searchable database of nationwide theater, music, opera, dance, film, and visual arts events. Online ticket purchase is available. The Arts Resources and Community link offers informative *CulturBriefs*—explanations of what all the fuss is about.

ART AND CRAFT SHOW DIRECTORY
http://artandcraftshows.net

Search through thousands of North American festivals where artisans and craftspeople display and sell their work. A state-by-state listing of the upcoming week's shows is included.

SEWING AND CRAFT EXPO
http://www.sewncraftexpo.com

AUSTRALIAN CRAFT SHOW
http://www.auscraft.com.au

FIESTA EN SANTA FE WEARABLE ART CONFERENCE
http://www.wearableart-conference.com

CRAFT PRODUCERS FINE ART AND CRAFT FESTIVALS
http://www.craftproducers.com

free Guides to Arts and Crafts Schools

No matter what your level of quilting ability, there are a variety of workshops available through arts and crafts schools and centers that can enhance your skills. Many offer intensive one- and two-week textile-related workshops—including quilt, fiber art, and surface design. The schools are often located in beautiful settings, with classes being taught by many nationally and internationally renowned instructors. In addition to learning, you get an opportunity to make new friends as you share classes, meals, and interests.

Be sure to visit **The Guide to Art and Craft Workshops** (**http://art.shawguides.com**) from Shaw Guides for the latest workshop information. You can search the database for a specific topic, view schools by state or country, or peruse categorized listings. Shaw Guides offers a free e-mail newsletter, *The Art and Craft Workshop Bulletin*, that you can sign up for at the site.

Shaw Guides offers free access to its continually updated comprehensive worldwide guides to creative programs.

ARROWMONT SCHOOL OF ARTS AND CRAFTS, GATLINBURG, TN
http://www.arrowmont.org

BROOKFIELD CRAFT CENTER, BROOKFIELD, CT
http://www.craftWeb.com/org/brookfld/brookfld.shtml

HAYSTACK MOUNTAIN SCHOOL OF CRAFTS, DEER ISLE, MAINE
http://www.haystack-mtn.org

PETERS VALLEY CRAFT CENTER, LAYTON, NJ
http://www.pvcrafts.org

PENLAND SCHOOL OF CRAFTS, PENLAND, NC
http://www.penland.org

COUPEVILLE ARTS CENTER, COUPEVILLE, WA
http://www.coupevillearts.org

CEDAR LAKES CRAFTS CENTER, RIPLEY, WV
http://www.cedarlakes.com/craftscenter.htm

GUILDFORD HANDCRAFT CENTER, GUILDFORD, CT
http://www.handcraftcenter.org

TOUCHSTONE CENTER FOR CRAFTS, FARMINGTON, PA
http://www.touchstonecrafts.com

THE JOHN C. CAMPBELL FOLK ART SCHOOL, BRASSTOWN, NC
http://www.folkschool.com

VALLEY FOLK ARTS, CARBONDALE, CO
http://www.valleyfolkarts.org
Includes information on the Quilting Retreat in the Rockies.

WOMEN'S STUDIO WORKSHOP, ROSENDALE, NY
http://www.wsworkshop.org

PRO CHEMICAL DYE VISITING ARTISTS WORKSHOPS, FALL RIVER, MA
http://www.prochemical.com
http://www.prochemical.com/classroom/visiting_artists_
   workshops.htm

CRAFTSUMMER, OXFORD, OH
http://www.muohio.edu/craftsummer

TEXTILE ARTS CENTRE, CHICAGO, IL
http://collaboratory.acns.nwu.edu/textilearts

THE SEWING WORKSHOP, SAN FRANCISCO, CA
http://www.sewingworkshop.com

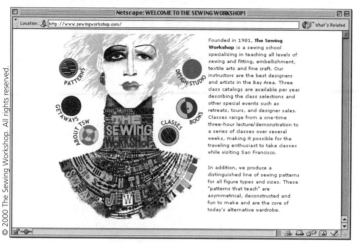

Netscape: WELCOME TO THE SEWING WORKSHOP!

Location: http://www.sewingworkshop.com/   What's Related

Founded in 1981, **The Sewing Workshop** is a sewing school specializing in teaching all levels of sewing and fitting, embellishment, textile arts and fine craft. Our instructors are the best designers and artists in the Bay Area. Three class catalogs are available per year describing the class selections and other special events such as retreats, tours, and designer sales. Classes range from a one-time three-hour lecture/demonstration to a series of classes over several weeks, making it possible for the traveling enthusiast to take classes while visiting San Francisco.

In addition, we produce a distinguished line of sewing patterns for all figure types and sizes. These "patterns that teach" are asymmetrical, deconstructed and fun to make and are the core of today's alternative wardrobe.

This school features sewing and surface design workshops and classes.

THE PRAIRIE SCHOOL OF TEXTILE ARTS, CARLINVILLE, IL
http://www.qhconline.com/ps-1.htm

**T
I
P**

Over 55? Visit Elderhostel—Adventures in Lifelong Learning (**http://www.elderhostel.org**), a not-for-profit organization committed to offering high-quality, affordable, educational opportunities to adults age 55 and over. Elderhostel offers thousands of diverse programs through colleges, museums, national parks, and learning centers. Select a catalog—U.S. and Canada, International (covering 85 countries), or Adventures Afloat. Then search through their special programs such as applied arts and crafts, or for a specific topic like quiltmaking, to view a list of opportunities.

how to Obtain Free Travel and Other Advice from Quilters

Wondering how much fabric you need to bring to a class taught by Nancy Crow? Looking for a roommate to share expenses at the International Quilt Festival in Houston? Curious as to whether there are any good places to eat in upper Spokane, Washington? One of the best ways to get answers to your questions is to ask other quilters. And often the best way to ask is through the Internet. By tapping into bulletin boards, chat rooms, newsgroups, or mailing lists, you can communicate with people from all over the world. No matter what time of day or night, someone, somewhere, is out there ready to reply. Information is shared. Questions are answered. Friendships are born.

• **Newsgroups.** Newsgroups are unmoderated public discussion forums, also called Usenet (for Users Network), on which you can post messages and reply to other users in a bulletin board fashion. Newsgroups are divided into major categories, called hierarchies—such as *rec* for recreation, *soc* for society and culture, and *biz* for business. Each hierarchy is followed by a period and a subcategory. For example, rec can include rec.art and rec.travel. There are thousands of subcategories, often containing further subcategories such as rec.travel.asia. To locate newsgroups, see the sites in this chapter.

In the past to participate in a newsgroup, you needed to install a newsreader (for example, **News Rover**, available for free at **http://www.newsrover.com**). Today the easiest way to participate in a newsgroup is to use **Deja.com Usenet Discussion Service** (**http://www.deja.com/usenet**) where you tap into messages directly from the Web. Additionally, your Web browser or AOL's software can be configured to "subscribe" to newsgroups. See your browser's online help or use AOL keyword Help for guidance.

Note that subscribing to a newsgroup can result in unwanted e-mail. For this reason, it's advisable to first obtain a free e-mail account—such as **Excite Mail** (**http://www.mailexcite.com**) or **Yahoo Mail** (**http://mail.yahoo.com**)—and use this address rather than your primary e-mail address for your newsgroups.

✋ *Warning! While there are many informative Usenet newsgroups devoted to traveling and quilting, they are unmoderated and uncensored. That means anything goes, including pornographic references.*

• **Chat.** A chat is a form of Internet communication that allows two or more people to have a real-time conversation. As you type and send your message, it is immediately relayed to those who are logged onto their computer and participating in the chat. A chat can take place on a Web page that supports a chat room or on an IRC channel. IRC stands for Internet Relay Chat, and it requires special software to participate. The software is generally free, and information on obtaining and configuring it is available from the Web site hosting the IRC chat.

• **E-Mail List.** An e-mail list is a forum in which participants subscribe to and receive messages by e-mail. More detailed information is included in this chapter.

• **Bulletin Board.** Bulletin boards (or message boards) are generally located on large Web sites. You can select a particular topic and read posted text messages. You can also reply to messages—either publicly or privately.

▩ *Free Directories to Newsgroups, Mailing Lists, and Chats*

DEJA.COM USENET DISCUSSION SERVICE
http://www.deja.com/usenet
You can read newsgroup postings directly through this Web site rather than through a traditional newsreader. Additionally, this site boasts the largest searchable archive of newsgroups and popular forums, too. To post to a newsgroup, you first need to register— but registration is free.

359 TRAVEL-RELATED NEWSGROUPS
http://www.sentex.net/~kramer/ici/Newsgroups.html

THE DIRECTORY OF PUBLICLY ACCESSIBLE MAILING LISTS
http://paml.net
Stephanie da Silva maintains this premier collection of mailing lists. An index and search engine are included.

META-LIST
http://www.meta-list.net
Search over 200,000 e-mail lists and newsletters.

LISZT—THE MAILING LIST DIRECTORY
http://www.Liszt.com
Liszt features a searchable database of over 90,000 mailing lists. You can also find discussion groups, newsgroups, and IRC chat.

E-GROUPS
http://www.egroups.com
Start an e-mail group or find one at this site featuring a searchable database and groups. A search on "quilt" revealed over 200 active mailing lists.

TILE NET
http://tile.net

FORUM ONE
http://www.forumone.com

Web Sites Offering Free Quilt-Related Mailing Lists

QUILTART HOSTED BY JUDY SMITH
http://www.quiltart.com

QUILTING MAILING LISTS FROM PLANET PATCHWORK
http://planetpatchwork.com/mailinglists.htm

DYERS LIST HOSTED BY PAT WILLIAMS
http://www.art.acad.emich.edu/lists/dyerslist/dyerslist.html

QUILTERS ONLINE RESOURCE CONNECTION MAILING LIST
http://www.nmia.com/~mgdesign/qor/index.html

QUILTROPOLIS
http://www.quiltropolis.net
http://www.quiltropolis.net/NewMailinglists.asp

This popular site is home to over 50 quilt, sewing, and fiber-related mailing lists and offers quick links for joining, getting a digest version of the list, and suspending delivery of a list while you're on vacation.

QUILTING AND OTHER MAILING LISTS FROM THE WIDE WORLD QUILTING PAGE
http://www.quilt.com/MailingListPage.html

QUILTERS BEE
http://www.quiltersbee.com

QUILTSWAPPERS
http://quiltswappers.tripod.com

NATIONAL ONLINE QUILTERS E-MAIL LISTS
http://noqers.org/lists.html

Web Sites Offering Free Bulletin Boards or Chats for Quilters

QUILTCHAT™
http://www.quiltchat.com

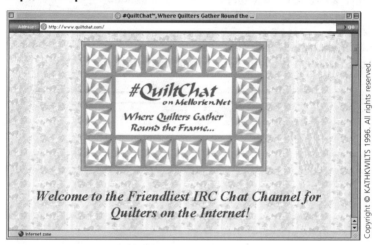

This site features regular IRC chats and "super" chats (chats with well-known quilting personalities) and online classes.

THE QUILTING FORUM BULLETIN BOARDS AT ABOUT.COM
http://quilting.about.com/hobbies/quilting/mpboards.htm

QUILT CHAT ROOM FOR QUILTING HOSTED BY SUSAN C. DRUDING AT ABOUT.COM
http://quilting.about.com/hobbies/quilting/mpchat.htm

DELPHI QUILTING ARTS FORUM
http://www.delphi.com/quilting

QUITROPOLIS QUILT CHAT
http://quiltropolis.com/chatcenter.htm

QUILTERS BEE
http://www.quiltersbee.com

FORUMS AT THE ARTS & CRAFTS SOCIETY
http://www.arts-crafts.com

YAHOO! CLUBS
http://clubs.yahoo.com
Visit Yahoo! Clubs and search for clubs to join, or start your own. The list of quilting clubs is growing. Here are two general clubs:

- **QUILTERS**
http://clubs.yahoo.com/clubs/quilters

- **THE QUILTING BEA**
http://clubs.yahoo.com/clubs/thequiltingbea

E-MAIL LISTS

A **mailing list** is a forum in which participants subscribe to and receive messages by e-mail.

Most e-mail lists are free, and you can subscribe to as many as you please. They come in two main flavors: announcement and discussion. **Announcement lists** are one-way and are mainly used to distribute information or news. **Discussion lists** are interactive, allowing the free exchange of messages among list members. These are the lists on which you can ask questions, share stories, and help others with advice.

E-mail discussion groups are moderated, unmoderated, open, or closed. Messages sent to a **moderated list** are first screened before being sent to everyone on the list. This is to keep the messages on topic and prevent "flame wars"—disruptive disagreements among list members. Messages to an **unmoderated list** are not screened. An **open list** welcomes anyone to join. A **closed list** can refer to different things, but it generally means you need approval by the list moderator to join. In most cases, a simple letter stating you want to join receives automatic approval.

E-mail lists are capable of producing a lot of e-mail—30, 40, even 100 or more messages daily. Unless you like that much e-mail, subscribe to a digest version of a list whenever available. A **digest** is a collection of 20 or more messages (depending on the message length) sent to you within a single e-mail.

To subscribe to any e-mail list, you first send a request to a list manager. Some Web sites make this very easy—you click a button and use an online form to subscribe, unsubscribe, suspend your mail while on vacation, or receive a digest of the list. Other Web sites for popular mail lists instruct you on how to e-mail the list manager. For example, you may send a message to <**listmanager@xyz.com**> and the body of your letter may say <**subscribe digest**>. Shortly after you subscribe, you will receive a welcome e-mail from the list manager. Save this important letter as it includes the e-mail address needed to send messages to everyone on the list, the general rules of the list, and instructions on how to unsubscribe from the list. Remember to send your subscribe and unsubscribe requests only to the list manager, not the entire group of subscribers.

Keep in mind that you don't have to participate in discussions when you join a list. You can simply read the messages. This is known as **lurking**. Often it's a good idea to lurk to get a sense of the group before posting. You may feel very comfortable with the list and jump into posting. Or, you may find the list isn't what you had in mind, in which case you can unsubscribe.

T I P

Want to chat with other woman travelers?

Subscribe to JourneyWoman's (**http://www.journeywoman.com**) HERmail.net (**http://www.HERmail.net**), a free e-mail service for women who want to talk to other women about travel. Currently there are over 3,000 women in 35 different countries who subscribe to the list.

NETIQUETTE

When posting to any Internet forum, it's important to know your netiquette—the rules of online etiquette. Here are some tips:

• Never send a file attachment (such as a picture of your quilt). Many servers cannot handle attachments.

• NEVER USE ALL CAPITALS in your message. It's hard to read and perceived as shouting.

• Never include personal information such as your address or phone number in a public list. Many lists are archived, meaning they are accessible long after you send it.

• Never forward warnings of computer viruses, pitches for donations, or other chain letters. These letters are almost always a hoax, and your well-meaning intention could result in your being blasted with angry e-mail, in addition to further circulating the hoax. See General Web Safety Tips in Chapter One for more info.

• Use a descriptive title in your subject line so your readers will know what your message is about.

• Send your message as text only, not as text and HTML (see your browser's preferences to correct).

• If a list pertains to a specific topic, keep your posts to that topic.

• If you're are replying to a particular message, copy the portion of the original message that you are responding to. Don't assume that everyone understands what you are replying to.

• Before sending your post, read it over carefully. Limit jokes and sarcasm, as they often do not translate well over an international audience. Remember that your message will linger for a long time in cyberspace.

• For more information on netiquette, visit **Dear Miss Emily Postnews (http://www.templetons.com/brad/emily.html)**, a humorous look at proper Net behavior written by Brad Templeton.

free Directories to Quilt Stores and Fabric

As little as five years ago, traveling to a new town meant scouring the Yellow Pages in search of quilt stores. Today most shops are listed on the Web—either on its own site or as part of a directory. By tapping into the Web before leaving home, you can learn about a store's hours, sales events, and the type of merchandise you can expect to find—even area attractions. Since many directories are constantly updated, you'll find new shops listed on the Web that are not yet listed in guide books. The sites in this chapter will help you locate the most up-to-date information on shops in your area or around the world. Once you locate the shops you want to visit during your travels, head over to Chapter 8 for sites offering free detailed directions and maps.

Even the Yellow Pages is online. Visit **Yellow Pages.com** (**http://www.yellowpages.com**) *to search on a particular category, such as fabric, quilt, or quilting. It generates a list within a 50 mile radius of your designated city and state. Or you can search an entire state. Other resources are also available.*

Free Directories to Quilt and Fabric Stores

ONLINE FABRIC DIRECTORY
http://www.fabdir.com

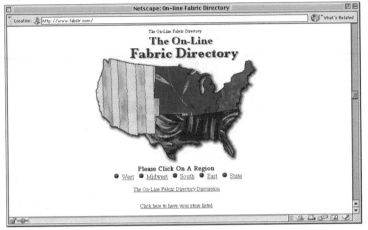

Click a region or state for an alphabetized listing of stores with addresses and phone numbers.

BETTER HOMES AND GARDENS QUILT DESTINATIONS
http://www.bhg.com/quiltvillage/destinations
Select a U.S. state or Canadian province to access shop listings, information, maps, and store links.

SHOP DIRECTORY OF THE QUILTER MAGAZINE
http://www.thequiltermag.com/shopdir.html
Locate quilt shops throughout the U.S., Canada, and England that sell The Quilter Magazine.

FABSHOP HOP—PARTICIPATING SHOPS BY STATE
http://www.fabshophop.com/listofshops.asp
Shops on this state-by-state list offer links to their Web sites.

JO-ANN FABRICS AND CRAFTS STORE LOCATOR
http://joann.com/store_locator/locator_main.html

QUILTSHOPS.COM
http://www.quiltshops.com

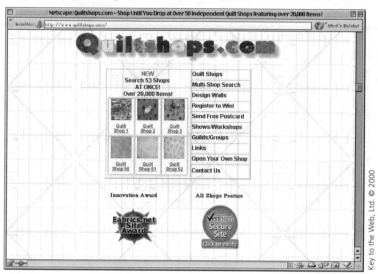

This site features a searchable database and a growing collection of fabric stores that offer online catalogs and shopping. Many of the shops offer extras, such as coupons you can print and present when visiting a store during your travels.

USA SHOPS FROM A–L,
FROM SUSAN C. DRUDING AT ABOUT.COM
http://quilting.about.com/hobbies/quilting/library/bl_shoplist.htm

USA SHOPS FROM M–W,
FROM SUSAN C. DRUDING AT ABOUT.COM
http://quilting.about.com/hobbies/quilting/library/
bl_shoplist-m-w.htm

Looking for directories to other needlework stores?
Visit The Caron Collection
(**http://caron-net.com/ordrshop.html**) for a directory of over 750 needlework stores located in the United States, Canada, Holland, UK, Norway, Australia, and New Zealand.

QUILT SHOP FIND FROM QUILTWOMAN.COM
http://www.quiltwoman.com/shop_fnd.cfm

© 2000 Ann Anderson

Ann Anderson's searchable database includes shops throughout the U.S. and in Australia, Canada, Denmark, Germany, Iceland, India, Spain, Sweden, and the UK.

LAZY GIRL DESIGNS—STORE GUIDE
http://www.lazygirldesigns.com/Store_Guide.htm
Looking for Lazy Girl Designs? See this comprehensive list.

THE QUILT CHANNEL—SHOPPING
http://www.quiltchannel.com/shopping
Links to general-purpose quilt stores, fabric stores, and more.

QUILT STORES
FROM THE WORLD WIDE QUILTING PAGE
http://www.quilt.com/QuiltStoresPage.html
Sue Traudt's directory updates immediately as new stores are added.

RAG SHOP STORE LOCATIONS
http://www.ragshop.com/locate.html

HANCOCK FABRICS STORE LOCATOR
http://www.hancockfabrics.com/store_locator.html

 *Free Directories from Fabric Manufacturers, Distributors, and Publishers*

Many of the top fabric manufacturers and distributors now include evolving directories of stores carrying their lines.

BALI FABRICS RETAIL OUTLETS
http://www.balifab.com

ULTIMATE DIRECTORY OF QUILT SHOPS
FROM C&T PUBLISHING
http://www.ctpub.com
A searchable directory to quilting, sewing, and craft shops is one of the features of this mega-site.

CHECKER DISTRIBUTORS
http://www.checkerdist.com/links/linkspage.html
Checkers offers a listing of states with links to independent quilt stores carrying items featured in their catalog.

Desperately seeking a special fabric to finish your project? Visit Missing Fabrics.com (**http://www.missingfabrics.com**) to place an ad to find that special piece of needed fabric, that out-of-print book, or the special sewing gizmo you purchased years ago. Or visit the site to see if you can help others in their quest.

P&B TEXTILES—LOCATE A SHOP NEAR YOU
http://www.pbtex.com/html/states.cfm

Learn about new fabric lines and what stores are carrying them.

SOUTH SEA IMPORTS—FIND A STORE NEAR YOU
http://www.southseaimports.com/fstore.htm

E.E. SCHENCK COMPANY
http://www.eeschenck.com
http://www.eeschenck.com/0/find_stores.asp
Use the "Where to Buy" search engine to find retail shops selling Andover Fabrics, Concord House, and Marcus Brothers fabrics.

HOFFMAN FABRICS RETAIL STORES
http://www.hoffmanfabrics.com/retailsrcs.html
Click on a state to see a list of stores carrying Hoffman Fabrics.

QUILT SHOP DIRECTORY FROM MARTINGALE
http://www.patchwork.com/office/ShopList.html
Quilt and craft shops organized by U.S. state and Canadian province. International shops are included.

RETAIL SHOPS CARRYING DEBBIE MUMM
http://www.debbiemumm.com/retail_outlet/retail_outlet.html

WHERE TO BUY RJR FABRICS
http://www.rjrfabrics.com/shops

Enter your zip code and the number of miles you are willing to travel. Presto—a list of stores, addresses, telephone numbers, and Web site URLs and e-mail addresses, if available, appears on your screen.

Looking for a discontinued RJR fabric? Visit **RJR Fabric Search** (**http://www.rjrfabrics.com/fabsearch/index.cfm**) to place a note on the Fabric Search bulletin board. Retailers can access the board and will respond if they have the fabric you're looking for.

Outlet stores are very popular with quilters. To learn where the best outlets are in the area of your travels, visit **Outlet Bound—The Internet Guide to Outlet Shopping** (**http://www.outletbound.com**) which details over 350 outlet malls throughout the country—including their stores, hours, directions, and general information.

Free Regional Directories of Quilt Shops

THE TRAVELING QUILTER FROM PLANET PATCHWORK
http://planetpatchwork.com/travel

Read charismatic and enlightening reviews of quilt shops.

- **QUILT SHOPS IN MARYLAND AND VIRGINIA**
http://www.planetpatchwork.com/passtvq/tvq41/index.htm

- **SAN FRANCISCO BAY AREA QUILT SHOPS**
http://planetpatchwork.com/sfbay.htm

- **QUILT SHOPS IN SOUTH LOUISIANA**
http://planetpatchwork.com/travel/neworleans.htm

- **QUILT SHOPS IN NORTH GEORGIA**
http://planetpatchwork.com/travel/northga.htm

- **QUILT SHOPS IN OHIO, KENTUCKY, AND TENNESSEE**
http://planetpatchwork.com/travel/ohkytn.htm

"Unless you like to make long treks only to find that the quilt store you thought was there, isn't, call ahead just before you depart. Even if you have what you believe is reliable information, shop hours change and shops move or go out of business. Store owners are always happy to provide out-of-towners with detailed directions on how to get to their place."

—Rob and Lynn Holland
Planet Patchwork (**http://www.planetpatchwork.com**)

Do you have a question about fabric?

Visit **Fabric Link** (**http://www.fabriclink.com**), a must-bookmark site. Kathy and Tom Swantko created and maintains this huge resource of unbiased educational information on fabrics. Learn about care and wear, what's in a label, and how to remove stains from fabric and carpets. Visit Fabric University for a history of fiber, the characteristics of textile fibers, fabric care 101, and much more.

PHOENIX AREA QUILT STORES (AZ)
http://www.primenet.com/~southpaw/phxshops.htm

SAN DIEGO COUNTY QUILT SHOPS (CA)
FROM ROSIE'S CALICO CUPBOARD
http://www.rosiescalicocupboard.com/areashops.html

"I recommend Rosie's Calico Cupboard *(***http://www.rosies calicocupboard.com***) to anyone looking for a good quilting store while visiting San Diego."*
   —Sarah Patrowicz (my talented sister-in-law), San Diego, CA

CONNECTICUT QUILTING STORES (CT)
http://users.neca.com/bobbi/qstore.html

MEMBER MERCHANTS FROM THE SUNSHINE STATE QUILTER'S ASSOCIATION (FL)
http://www.ssqa.org/merchant.htm

ATLANTA AREA QUILT SHOPS (GA)
http://www.mindspring.com/~quilts/shops.htm

HAWAIIAN QUILT STORE DIRECTORY (HI)
http://www.nvo.com/poakalani/usefullinks
Shop directory courtesy of Hawaiian Quilting with Poakalani & Co.

ILLINOIS QUILT AND FABRIC STORES (IL)
http://www.prairienet.org/quilts/stores.html

HANCOCK'S OF PADUCAH (KY)
http://www.hancocks-paducah.com

BAZAAR DEL MUNDO (CA)
http://www.bazaardelmundo.com

I visited this delightful place located in Old Country San Diego, California at the recommendation of Yvonne Porcella. Vibrant colors and fragrant flora abound; unique gifts are aplenty. Be sure to visit Fabrics & Finery where you'll find a bold colorful fabrics, trims, and ribbons from around the world. An annual Fabric Fantasies Festival is held in June.

MASSACHUSETTS QUILT SHOPS (MA)

http://www.nlqg.org/ma_quilt_shops.html

MAINE AND NEW HAMPSHIRE QUILT SHOPS (MA AND NH)

http://www.mainequilts.org/Fabric_shops.htm

NEW HAMPSHIRE QUILT SHOPS (NH)

http://www.nlqg.org/nh_quilt_shops.html

QUILT SHOPS IN NEW JERSEY (NJ)

http://www.njquilts.org

NEW YORK CITY SHOPPING LOCATIONS FOR FABRIC LOVERS (NY)

http://users.ids.net/~rounds/newyork.html

LANCASTER COUNTY, PENNSYLVANIA RESOURCES FOR QUILTERS (PA)

http://www.quiltart.com/lancaster.html

Judy Smith shares a comprehensive resource of quilt shops in Lancaster County, complete with directions and area attractions.

HOUSTON AREA QUILT SHOPS FROM THE QUILT GUILD OF GREATER HOUSTON (TX)

http://www.geocities.com/~qggh/main/shops.html

Visit other fabric manufacturer sites online to learn about their fabric lines.

FABRIC TRADITIONS
http://www.fabrictraditions.com

KONA BAY FABRICS
http://www.konabay.com

MARCUS BROTHERS TEXTILES INC.
http://www.marcusbrothers.com

SALSA FABRICS
http://www.salsafabrics.com

VIRGINIA QUILT SHOPS (VA)
http://www.vcq.org/shops.htm

VERMONT QUILT SHOPS (VT)
http://www.nlqg.org/vt_quilt_shops.html

QUILTING SHOPS IN WASHINGTON STATE (WA)
http://www.wasiq.org

WEST VIRGINIA QUILT SHOPS (WV)
http://www.wvquilters.org/Quiltshops.html

KEEPSAKE QUILTING (NH)
http://www.keepsakequilting.com

Judy B. Dales recommends a visit to Keepsake Quilting anytime one is in New Hampshire.

"There is not a lot of frou-frou—just lots of fabric, efficient help, and plenty of space for looking at said fabric." When visiting the site, be sure to request a catalog.

© Keepsake Quilting, Inc.

🪡 NEW YORK CITY SHOPPING, BY JOHN SWIATEK

The Garment District, showrooms, design rooms, and some light manufacturing are centered around 7th Avenue, from 35th Street to 40th Street.

Fabric shopping opportunities are most found between 7th and 8th, including 8th Avenue—which can have some of the cheesiest things you will ever want to see. If you LOOK like a tourist, be particularly careful with all your money. Many fabric bolts do not include fiber content. Some vendors will tell you whatever it is they think you want to hear. In all cases, trust your fingers, and know your fabrics.

Leathers, suedes, and furs are between 6th and 7th, south of Penn Station. But the largest selection of Ultrasuede® is at B&J Fabrics, on 40th near 8th Avenue. B&J has the widest selection of all types of fabrics, and is a great first stop. Many other vendors specialize in particular types of fabric.

Sewing notions and supplies can be found at Steinlauf & Stoller on West 39th Street between 7th and 8th, but there are other similar stores in that area. Shops selling industrial sewing machines and ironing supplies are also nearby.

Trimmings and embellishment shopping is between 5th Avenue and 6th Avenue, from 36th to 39th Street. Find extraordinary ribbons at Hyman Hendler on 38th Street— with extraordinary prices. There are more trimming shops

Looking for online suppliers? The Buyer's Index for Sewing, Fabrics, and Textiles (**http://www.buyersindex.com/brca/42.htm**) features a searchable database of fabrics, lace, books, threads, and other supplies.

springing up between 7th and 8th, but west of 7th, they seem to carry oddlots and closeouts on trims.

There are almost always some kind of sample sales going on, somewhere. Be leery. Evaluate the looks of the person handing out the flyers. If there is a line someplace, and they look like people you might want to know, chances are it is your kind of sample sale. A carefully painted sandwich-board sign is a give-away that the sample sale is not what it promises to be.

—John Swiatek
Parsons School of Design
New York City, NY

The following sites will assist you in your travel around New York City:

• **NY.COM—THE PAPERLESS GUIDE TO NYC**
(**http://www.ny.com**) Including extensive information on sightseeing, shopping, museums, restaurants, maps, and more.

• **THE NEW YORK CITY INSIDER**
(**http://www.theinsider.com/nyc**) Includes a guide to NYC museums, restaurants, sights, and attractions.

• **METROPOLITAN TRANSPORTATION AUTHORITY**
(**http://www.mta.nyc.ny.us**) Contains information covering NYC Transit, Long Island Railroad, Long Island Bus, Metro-North Railroad, and bridges and tunnels.

• **NYC TRANSIT SUBWAY SCHEDULE**
(**http://www.mta.nyc.ny.us/nyct/service/fline.htm**)

T I P

Looking for more information on fabric?

How to Identify Fabric (**http://www.fabrics.net/fabricsr.htm**) and Fabric Information and Facts (**http://www.fabrics.net/fabricinfo.htm**) from Fabrics.net (**http://www.fabricsnet.com**) will answer your questions.

Free Directories to Quilt Shops Worldwide

QUILTING AROUND THE WORLD
LISTING OF INTERNATIONAL SHOPS FROM SUSAN C. DRUDING AT ABOUT.COM
http://quilting.about.com/hobbies/quilting/library/
  bl_shoplist-intl.htm

QUILT STORES IN EUROPE
FROM THE WORLD WIDE QUILTING PAGE
http://www.quilt.com/Stores/Europe/Europe.html

QUILT STORES IN AUSTRALIA AND NEW ZEALAND
FROM THE WORLD WIDE QUILTING PAGE
http://www.quilt.com/Stores/Australia/Australia.html

QUILT STORES IN ASIA
FROM THE WORLD WIDE QUILTING PAGE
http://www.quilt.com/Stores/Asia/Asia.html

QUILT SOURCE CANADA
http://www.quiltsource.ca

FABRIC/QUILT STORES IN NOVA SCOTIA, CANADA
http://www.chebucto.ns.ca/~ae862/ns_stores.html

QUILT SHOPS IN EUROPE
http://home2.inet.tele.dk/ynielsen/europeshops.htm

QUILTING STORES IN THE UK
http://www.quiltingdirectory.co.uk/shops.htm

LONDON AREA QUILT SHOPS
http://members.tripod.co.uk/London_Quilters/londonshops.htm

QUILT STORES IN FRANCE
http://www.quiltcreations.com/eng/stores.htm

To locate ATMs worldwide, visit these sites:
- **MASTERCARD ATM LOCATOR**
http://www.mastercard.com/atm/
- **VISA ATM LOCATOR**
http://www.visa.com/pd/atm/main.html
- **CITIBANK ATM/BRANCH LOCATIONS**
http://www.citibank.com/branches

BEST IN MOSCOW—FABRICS, SEWING NOTIONS
http://www.infoservices.com/moscow/355.htm

AUSTRALIAN QUILT STORES
FROM DOWN UNDER QUILTS ONLINE
http://www.duquilts.com.au/market.htm

NEW ZEALAND QUILT STORES
FROM NZ QUILTERS ONLINE
http://www.nzquilter.org.nz/mall/mmall/default.htm

DUTCH QUILT SHOPS FROM THE BLAZING STARS
http://www.dse.nl/blazingstars/shops.htm

QUILTING SUPPLIES FROM CAPE TOWN,
SOUTH AFRICA
http://www.handmade.co.za/quilting/index.html
Check the Rendezvous link for a list of South African quilting guilds, shows, and other happenings of interest to quilters.

free Information on Quilting Guilds and Associations

The Web makes the world one big quilting bee. We can tap in and chat with quilters from all corners of the globe. But quilters love meeting face-to-face, sharing new techniques, show and tell, and the latest quilting gossip. That's why guilds continue to be so popular. Use the Web to find a quilting guild or association in your home state or wherever your travels take you. Start by searching some of the large directories. Many contain online registration forms making it easy for new guilds to be added on a regular basis. Be sure to visit the Web page of a guild or two in the area of your travel destination. Many offer lists of regional shops, area shows, and attractions on their sites, and all will welcome you as a guest to their meetings.

Free Directories to Quilting Guilds

QUILTING GUILDS AROUND THE WORLD FROM THE WORLD WIDE QUILTING PAGE
http://www.quilt.com/QuiltGuildsPage.html
Sue Traudt's directory includes guilds throughout the U.S, Canada, Austria, France, Germany, Sweden, and Australia.

QUILT GUILD LIST FROM McCALL'S QUILTING
http://www.mccallsquilting.com/mccalls/guilds.htm
A state-by-state list with guild names, addresses, meeting information, and e-mail addresses and URLs, if available.

QUILTING GUILDS AND ASSOCIATIONS FROM ABOUT.COM
http://quilting.about.com/hobbies/quilting/msubguild.htm
From Susan C. Druding, quilting host at About.com.

QUILT GUILDS WORLDWIDE
http://www.quiltguilds.com

Hickory Hill Quilts (**http://www.hickoryhillquilts.com**) hosts this wonderful directory where you'll find information on guilds for each state in the U.S., Canada, Guam, Japan, France, South Africa, and other countries around the world.

QUILT GUILDS AND ASSOCIATIONS FROM LOSTQUILT.COM
http://www.lostquilt.com/LostQuiltLinks5.html
Maria Elkins maintains a list of online, regional, and international quilt guilds.

QUILT GUILDS FROM QUILTSHOPS.COM
http://www.quiltshops.com/groups.htm
A searchable database of quilt guilds and groups.

DAWN DUPERAULT'S QUILT GUILDS ONLINE
http://www.RedDawn.net/quilt/guilds.htm

QUILT GUILDS FROM QUILTCHAT™
http://www.quiltchat.com/guilds/index.html

AFRICAN AMERICAN QUILT GUILDS
http://quiltethnic.com/guilds.html

C&T'S ULTIMATE DIRECTORY OF GUILDS AND GROUPS
http://www.ctpub.com

QUILTING GUILDS SEARCH ENGINE FROM QUILTWOMAN.COM
http://www.quiltwoman.com/guild_fnd.cfm

Ann Anderson maintains this growing searchable database with guild infor-mation for the 50 states, Canada, Belgium, Brazil, German, NSW Australia, Saudi Arabia, and Spain.

> **TIP**
> AOL users, head to Keyword: **Quilt**
> and then select *Quilters Resources* where you'll
> find an organized directory of shops, shows, guilds,
> and more.

> **TIP**
> If you can't find the
> perfect pillow or organizer
> needed for your trip, try
> Travel Accessories.com
> (**http://www.travelaccessories.com**).

WEBRINGS

A WebRing is a collection of sites linked together by a common theme to form a circle. Traveling a Ring is a great way to discover related sites without having to weed through the quagmire of search engine results. Like jumping from horse to horse on a merry-go-round, you travel a Ring by clicking a navigation link within the Ring's graphic, usually found on the bottom of a member site. Some Rings allow you to view all of the linked sites, others allow you to view five sites a a time, or you can click "next" and travel the ring until you end up where you started. You don't have to be a member of the ring to travel it, and Web rings are free.

The best way to discover WebRings for quilters and travel is to visit WebRing (**http://www.webring.org**), a master directory of Web Rings. Here are two rings dedicated to quilt guilds.

QUILT GUILD WEB RING
http://www.millcomm.com/~quilt/guild.htm

THE CANADIAN QUILTER'S WEB RING
http://www.crosswinds.net/~canadaquilting

Next
Skip Next
Previous
List Sites
Join us!
the Canadian
Quilter's WebRing

© 2000 Jenn Callum

Free Information on Local Quilting Guilds

ANCHORAGE LOG CABIN QUILTERS (AK)
http://www.alaskaquilts.org

ARIZONA QUILTING GUILD (AZ)
http://www.accessarizona.com/community/groups/azquiltersguild

TUCSON QUILTER'S GUILD (AZ)
http://iwhome.com/quilter

FOLSOM QUILT & FIBER GUILD (CA)
http://www.folsomquilt.org

NITE OWL QUILTERS GUILD IN UPLAND, CALIFORNIA (CA)
http://home.earthlink.net/~wlsrkeeling/noqg.htm

CONEJO VALLEY QUILTERS IN VENTURA COUNTY (CA)
http://members.aol.com/cvqinca

PIECEMAKERS BY THE SEA IN HALF MOON BAY (CA)
http://www.coastside.net/margie

CANYON QUILTERS OF SAN DIEGO (CA)
http://www.sandiego.com/quilt

FRIENDSHIP QUILTERS OF SAN DIEGO (CA)
http://friendship.quilt.to

CONNECTICUT QUILTING DIGEST AND GUILDS (CT)
http://users.neca.com/bobbi

LADYBUG QUILTERS IN NEWARK, DELAWARE (DE)
http://www.dca.net/ladybugsquilt

Visit **Quit Magic** by Carolyn Hill (**http://ecuador.junglevision.com/carolyn/qhp.htm**) to read inspiring stories about quilts and quiltmakers.

Award-winning textile artist **Caryl Bryer Fallert** offers valuable information on her **Quilt Care** (**http://www.bryerpatch.com/faq/storage.htm**) page where she answers storage, hanging, and shipping questions.

CENTRAL FLORIDA QUILTER'S GUILD (FL)
http://www.insidecentralflorida.com/community/groups/
   QuilterGuild

SUNSHINE STATE QUILTERS ASSOCIATION (FL)
http://www.ssqa.org

QUILT ATLANTA (GA)
http://www.mindspring.com/~quilts/index.htm

ATLANTA AREA QUILT GUILDS (GA)
http://www.mindspring.com/~quilts/guilds.htm

HAWAIIAN QUILT GUILDS (HI)
FROM HAWAIIAN QUILTING WITH POAKALANI & CO.
http://www.nvo.com/poakalani/quiltguilds

QUILT GUILDS IN ILLINOIS (IL)
http://www.prairienet.org/quilts/guilds.html

ILLINI COUNTRY STITCHERS QUILT GUILD (IL)
http://www.prairienet.org/quilts

KAW VALLEY QUILTER'S GUILD (KA)
http://community.lawrence.com/KawValleyQuiltersGuild

MINNESOTA QUILTERS (MN)
http://www.quiltersguildofdallas.org

OZARKS PIECEMAKERS QUILT GUILD (MO)
http://www.orion.org/~opqg

FRIENDSHIP STAR QUILTERS GUILD (MD)
http://www.friendshipstar.org

THE STATE GUILD OF NJ, INC. (NJ)
http://www.njquilts.org
Includes a directory of local NJ guilds.

NEW MEXICO QUILTING ASSOCIATION (NM)
http://www.nmqa.nm.org

ASHEVILLE QUILT GUILD (NC)
http://www.main.nc.us/AQG

NORTHERN NIGHTS QUILT GUILD (NH)
http://www.nlqg.org

EMPIRE QUILTERS GUILD (NY)
http://www.empirequilters.org

QUILTERS OF COLOR NETWORK OF NEW YORK, INC. (NY)
http://members.tripod.com/~QCN

EMERALD VALLEY QUILTERS GUILD (OR)
http://www.efn.org/~evq

UNDERCOVER QUILTERS (BROOKHAVEN, PA)
http://undercoverquilters.home.att.net

SMOKY MOUNTAIN QUILTERS OF TENNESSEE (TN)
http://www.korrnet.org/smq/show2000.htm

AUSTIN AREA QUILT GUILD (TX)
http://www.aaqg.org

THE QUILTER'S GUILD OF DALLAS (TX)
http://www.quiltersguildofdallas.org

LAKEVIEW QUILTER'S GUILD (TX)
http://www.lakeviewquiltersguild.org

LAND O'LAKES QUILT GUILD (TX)
http://www.lewisville.com/nporgs/lol

SAN ANTONIO QUILT GUILD (TX)
http://www.sanantonioquilt.org

QUILT GUILD OF GREATER HOUSTON (TX)
http://www.geocities.com/~qggh

QUILTERS UNLIMITED IN NORTHERN VIRGINIA (VA)
http://www.quiltersunlimited.org

VIRGINIA QUILT GUILDS (VA)
http://www.vcq.org/guild.htm

WASHINGTON STATE INTERNET QUILTERS (WA)
http://www.wasiq.org
Includes a directory of guilds across Washington state.

LACROSSE AREA QUILTERS (WI)
http://www.geocities.com/~lacrossequilt

WEST VIRGINIA QUILTERS, INC. (WV)
http://www.wvquilters.org

Visit QuiltEthnic.Com (**http://www.quiltethnic.com**) for a fascinating look at the textile traditions of African, Haitian, African-American, Latin American, Asian, and Native American ethnic groups.

Free Information on Guilds Around the World

COMMON THREADS QUILT GUILD CANADA
http://www.commonthread.on.ca

NOVA SCOTIA GUILD, CANADA
http://www.chebucto.ns.ca/~ae862/ns_quilt.html

EUROPEAN QUILT ASSOCIATION
http://eqa.homepage.dk

**FRENCH QUILTERS' GUILD SITE
FROM FRANCE PATCHWORK**
http://www.francepatchwork.com/english_homepage.htm

**BLACK FOREST QUILT GUILD IN STUTTGART,
GERMANY**
http://dreamwater.com/bfqguild

ASSOCIATION OF SWISS QUILTERS
http://www.patchquilt.ch

QUILT ITALIA
http://www.goldnet.it/quiltitalia/indexeng.html

BELGIUM PATCHWORK ASSOCIATION
http://www.belgiumquilt.be

DIRECTORY OF QUILT GUILDS IN THE UK
http://www.quiltingdirectory.co.uk/groups.htm

THE LONDON QUILTERS
http://members.tripod.co.uk/London_Quilters/lq1.htm

**THE QUILTER'S GUILD OF THE BRITISH ISLES—
REGION ONE (LONDON)**
http://www.qgr1.freeserve.co.uk

SCANDINAVIA ART QUILT GROUP
http://home5.swipnet.se/~w-58758

NEW ZEALAND QUILTERS ONLINE
http://nzquilter.org.nz

THE QUILTERS' GUILD IN SYDNEY, AUSTRALIA
http://www.ozemail.com.au/~quiltgld

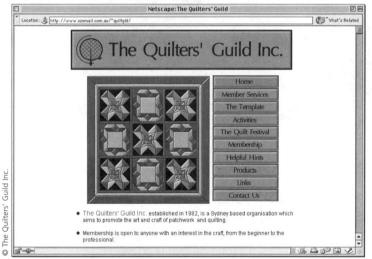

QUILT GROUP MEETINGS AND CONTACTS
IN NSW AUSTRALIA
http://www.shoal.net.au/~nbray/group.html

WEST AUSTRALIAN QUILTER'S ASSOCIATION, INC.
http://members.tripod.com/waqa

AUSTRALIAN QUILT GUILDS FROM DOWN UNDER QUILTS ONLINE
http://www.duquilts.com.au

Free Information on Quilting Associations

AMERICAN QUILTER'S SOCIETY
http://www.AQSquilt.com

You'll find information on membership, the Society's museum, and the esteemed annual AQS quilt show at this site.

INTERNATIONAL QUILT ASSOCIATION
http://www.quilts.org/iqa.htm
Learn about membership benefits, including entry information to the renowned Quilts: A World of Beauty *show.*

THE ALLIANCE FOR AMERICAN QUILTS
http://www.quilts.org/alliance.htm

THE NATIONAL QUILTING ASSOCIATION, INC.
http://www.NQAQuilts.org

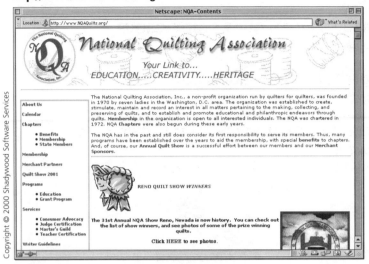

THE CANADIAN QUILTER'S ASSOCIATION
http://members.tripod.com/~cqaacc

STUDIO ART QUILT ASSOCIATES
http://www.saqa.com

CONTEMPORARY QUILT ART ASSOCIATION
http://www.contemporaryquiltart.com

THE CRAZY QUILT SOCIETY
http://www.crazyquilt.com

ASSOCIATION OF PACIFIC NORTHWEST QUILTERS (APNQ)
http://www.apnq.org

QUILT VISIONS—THE ART OF THE QUILT
http://www.quiltvisions.orp
Learn about Quilt San Diego, a not-for-profit organization dedicated to the promotion of quilts as art, and the prestigious Visions quilt show.

THE ARTQUILT NETWORK
http://www.adkey.com/aqn

THE AMERICAN QUILT STUDY GROUP
http://www2.h-net.msu.edu/aqsg

HOME SEWING ASSOCIATION
http://www.sewing.org.

INTERNATIONAL MACHINE QUILTERS ASSOCIATION
http://imqa.org

THE NATIONAL CRAFT ASSOCIATION
http://www.craftassoc.com

INTERNATIONAL SEWING MACHINE COLLECTORS SOCIETY
http://www.ismacs.net

FRIENDS OF FIBER ART INTERNATIONAL
http://206.204.3.133/dir_nii/nii_dat_fiber.html
(Through The Penny Nii Collection at **http://www.penny-nii.com***)*

ALLIANCE OF ARTISTS COMMUNITIES
http://www.artistcommunities.org

THE APPLIQUÉ SOCIETY
http://www.theappliquésociety.org

SEATTLE TEXTILE COMPUTER USERS GROUP
http://www.wolfenet.com/~workshop/stcug

AMERICAN SEWING GUILD
http://www.asg.org

If you have lost a quilt, or found one and are trying to locate its rightful owner, visit the **Lost Quilt Page** (**http://www.lostquilt.com**). The site includes excellent information such as documenting your quilts, shipping your quilts safely, displaying your quilts away from home, and resolving problems with UPS. Also try **Quilts Lost and Found** (**http://www2.succeed.net/~amc/quilts.html**).

free Guides to Quilt Shows, Contests, Competitions and Exhibitions

You've worked on it for weeks, even months—sometimes years. You're intimate with its every stitch, its every nuance. Finally the day arrives when it—your latest quilted work of art— is finished and ready for display. Rather than paging through piles of old magazines looking for places to exhibit, tap into the Web for the latest quilt show and exhibition news. The sites in this chapter will help you find the perfect venue to display your quilted creations, and having your quilt on display will give you ample reason to travel to yet another show.

For more quilt show information, visit Chapters 14 and 16.

🛒 FIBER ART NEWS AND EVENTS CALENDAR FROM DHARMA TRADING CO.
http://www.dharmatrading.com/events
Learn about classes, shows, fairs, textile-related jobs, and internships on this searchable database for fiber artists and textile craftspersons.

QUILT SHOWS FROM QUILT GUILDS WORLDWIDE
http://www.quiltguilds.com/addss.htm
Click on a month and learn what shows are happening worldwide. The site includes a registration form to list your event.

QUILT SHOW LIST FROM QUILTCHAT™
http://www.quiltchat.com/shows/index.html
A month-by-month listing of shows and a handy form to include your show.

CONTESTS FROM QUILTMAKER MAGAZINE
http://www.quiltmaker.com/qm/contest.htm

QUILTER'S NEWSLETTER MAGAZINE
http://www.quiltersnewsletter.com/qnm

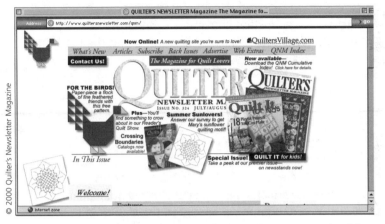

Quilter's Newsletter Magazine generously shares its contest and quilting event news on its Web site. Here's what you can find:

• CONTESTS IN THE NEWS
http://www.quiltersvillage.com/qnm/contest.htm
Learn the latest contest opportunities.

• CALENDAR OF EVENTS
http://www.quiltersvillage.com/qnm/calendar.htm
Quilt show information is provided by show organizers. The directory is divided by U.S. states and includes listings for over 15 countries.

• IT'S SHOWTIME
http://www.quiltersvillage.com/qnm/showtime.htm
A month-by-month listing of shows and events.

QUILT TOWN BULLETIN BOARD
FROM CHITRA PUBLICATIONS
http://www.quilttownusa.com/Visitors_Center/bullboard.asp
Visit Quilt Shows for a listing by state and Quilt Events for a listing in date order.

QUILT SHOW LIST FROM McCALL'S QUILTING
http://www.quiltersvillage.com/mccalls/showlist.htm
A month-by-month listing of quilt shows with contact information.

When entering a show outside the U.S., the quilt size is often required in centimeters rather than inches. For an instant conversion, visit **Unitwiz** (**http://www.unitwiz.com**). Fill in a form, and the program calculates and displays the conversion.

Looking to showcase your quilts in art galleries and festivals?
Visit **Art Calendar's Online Art Organization Listings** (**http://www.artcalendar.com/netlistings/default.html**)
Click on a geographical region on the U.S. map to see listings for organizations in that area. Many groups are dedicated to the development of textile artists.

DAVID WALKER'S BULLETIN BOARD
http://w3.one.net/~davidxix/Pages/BulletinBoard.html
Among other things, David details exhibition opportunities, current exhibits and events, and information on traveling exhibits.

QUILT SHOW SEARCH ENGINE
FROM QUILTWOMAN.COM
http://www.quiltwoman.com/show_fnd.cfm
One-button access to All Shows, Guild Shows, or Non-Guild Shows in this searchable database from Ann Anderson.

QUILT SHOWS AROUND THE UK
FROM GROSVENOR HOUSE PUBLISHING
http://www.grosvenor-publishing.co.uk
The publisher of Fabrications offers quilt show information, including National Quilt Championships, Ardingly Quilt Festival, and Chilford Quilt Festival.

SHOWS/WORKSHOPS FROM QUILT SHOP.COM
http://www.quiltshops.com/events.htm
Search by state or view all the shows and workshops registered.

STUDIO ART QUILT ASSOCIATION—
CONFERENCES, WORKSHOPS, AND EVENTS
http://www.saqa.com/Calendar.html
Learn the latest info, including extensive museum and gallery exhibition information.

QUILT SHOWS IN HAWAII
FROM HAWAIIAN QUILTING WITH POAKALANI & CO.
http://www.nvo.com/poakalani/quiltshows

What are the best ways to ship a quilt?

Some people are more comfortable with one service than another. I prefer Federal Express 2nd day or insured UPS. Whatever courier service you use, be sure to obtain a tracking number. You can then plug the tracking number into the company's Web site to follow your quilt's journey and confirm its safe arrival.

• **FEDERAL EXPRESS**
http://www.fedex.com

• **UNITED PARCEL SERVICE**
http://www.ups.com

• **U.S. POSTAL SERVICE**
http://www.usps.gov

• **DHL WORLDWIDE EXPRESS**
http://www.dhl.com

• **ISHIP BY STAMPS.COM**
http://www.iship.com/priceit/price.asp
Check this site to find the best rates. Enter the package weight, origin, and destination. iShip will then generate a comparison of delivery costs.

EVENTS:
COMPETITIONS & CHALLENGES FROM ABOUT.COM
http://quilting.about.com/hobbies/quilting/msubevent.htm

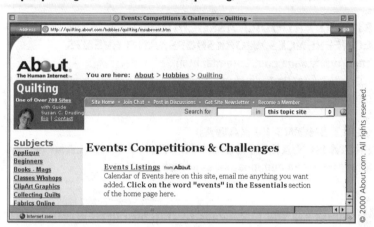

Susan C. Druding maintains this informative list which includes related links.

QUILT SHOWS AROUND THE WORLD
FROM THE WORLD WIDE QUILTING PAGE
http://www.quilt.com/QuiltShowsPage.html
Divided by geographical location, learn about upcoming shows throughout the country and around the world. Links to quilt show reviews and show information are included at this site from Sue Traudt.

FLORIDA QUILT SHOWS FROM SSQA
http://www.ssqa.org/qltshows.htm

QUILT SHOWS IN THE MIDWEST
http://www.prairienet.org/quilts/shows.html

VIRGINIA QUILT SHOWS
http://www.vcq.org/calendar.htm

NEW JERSEY QUILT SHOW DIRECTORY
http://www.njquilts.org

free Guides to National and International Quilt Shows and Festivals

Walking into a large quilt show is like entering an enchanted universe where everything that exists is there to please quilters. There are hundreds of magnificent quilts displayed for your perusal and hordes of vendors offering a potpourri of quilting fabrics and goods—giving the term "shop till you drop" new meaning. Shows often run for several days, allowing you time to experience the delights and take a few classes, too. Attending such a show can make you feel vibrantly alive and proud to call yourself a quiltmaker. And should you discover your quilt adorned with a ribbon, all the world is aglow.

While large shows are invigorating, they are also exhausting. Wear comfortable walking shoes or sneakers, clothes in layers, and bring a pull tote with wheels to haul around your goods. Take hourly breaks for stretching and drinking water to give your body a chance to recharge itself. If time permits, take a day to visit area attractions—you'll find some favorites included below.

The sites in this chapter offer the latest show news, including class information and entry forms, so that even if you can't make it to the show, maybe your quilt can.

INTERNATIONAL QUILT FESTIVAL
HOUSTON, TX—NOVEMBER
http://www.quilts.com
Called "The World's Fair of Quilts," this event is huge!

"I rent an economy car and stay at an Extended Stay America *(**http://www.extendedstay.com**) spot for a week (a week stay offers the lowest rate). Each room includes a complete kitchen, where I eat my daily breakfast and some dinners.*

You can park for $2–$3 per day in lots right next to the convention center. Having a car gives the mobility for sightseeing, etc.

For lunch I walk outside and around the back of the George Brown Convention Center. This is about a 3 block walk. There is a 'Vietnamese Town' there with many Vietnamese restaurants with great food and very reasonable prices."

—Nancy Eha (**http://www.beadcreative.com**)
St. Paul, MN

Visit the **Galleria** area of Houston for incredible shopping. From the George Brown Convention Center, you 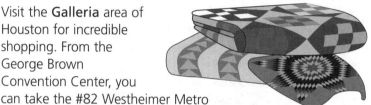 can take the #82 Westheimer Metro bus to the Galleria Shopping Center. For more information on buses and schedules, see **Metro Bus Schedule and Route Maps (http://www.ridemetro.org/SERVMENU.HTM)**.

A favorite area attraction of mine is the **Houston Zoo** (**http://www.houstonzoo.org**). My husband and I think it's one of the best zoos in the country, and the admission price is surprisingly inexpensive—$2.50 per person the last time we visited.

If you have a car and like gardens, consider visiting the **Moody Gardens (http://www.moodygardens.com)** in nearby Galveston. Tap into **Galveston Island** (**http://www.galveston.com**) for information on attractions in Galveston, such as its gorgeous historic homes.

Also see:

• **THE OFFICIAL GUIDE TO HOUSTON**
http://www.houston-guide.com

• **TEXAS—TRAVEL, TOURISM, AND RECREATION**
http://www.state.tx.us/Travel

• **HOUSTON AREA QUILT SHOPS**
FROM THE QUILT GUILD OF GREATER HOUSTON
http://www.geocities.com/~qggh/main/shops.html
AMERICAN QUILTER'S SOCIETY SHOW
PADUCAH, KY—APRIL
http://www.aqsquilt.com

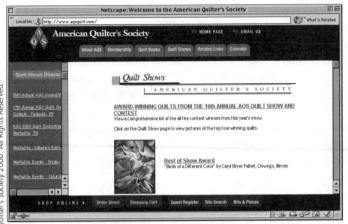

When in Paducah, be sure to visit the Museum of the American Quilter's Society (http://quiltmuseum.org) where you can view past Best of Show winners of the prestigious AQS show.

Also see:

• **PADUCAH, KENTUCKY VISITORS CENTER**
http://www.paducah-tourism.org

• **WEST KENTUCKY TOURISM**
http://www.westkentucky.com

• **PADUCAHKY.COM**
http://www.paducahky.com/paducah.html

THE VERMONT QUILT FESTIVAL
NORWICH UNIVERSITY, NORTHFIELD, VT—JULY
http://www.vqf.org

See also:

• **WELCOME TO NORTHFIELD, VERMONT**
http://www.in-vermont.com/northfield

• **DISCOVER VERMONT**
http://www.discover-vermont.com

• **VERMONT QUILT SHOPS**
http://www.nlqg.org/vt_quilt_shops.html

QUILTERS HERITAGE CELEBRATION
LANCASTER, PA—LATE MARCH, EARLY APRIL
http://www.qhconline.com

"In addition to all the quilt-related shops, quilters should check out The People's Place Museum *(http://www.the peoplesplace.com) located across the street from The Old Country Store in Intercourse. The People's Place is an educational and heritage center about the Amish and the Mennonites and gives a great overview of life in Lancaster County. In addition,* The People's Place Quilt Museum *(http://www.ppquiltmuseum.com) is located upstairs from The Old Country Store and offers changing exhibits of antique Amish and Mennonite quilts (usually pre-1940) and other decorative arts.*

When you get tired of quilts and antiquing, Lancaster County is a shopper's paradise, with two huge top-notch, upscale outlet malls on Route 30."

—Judy Smith, Washington, D.C.

Also see:

• **JUDY SMITH'S LANCASTER, PA RESOURCES FOR QUILTERS**
http://www.quiltart.com/lancaster.html

• **THE PENNSYLVANIA DUTCH COUNTRY WELCOME CENTER**
http://www.PennsylvaniaDutchCountry.com

• **AMISH COUNTY TOURIST BUREAU**
http://www.amish.net

MID-ATLANTIC QUILT FESTIVAL
WILLIAMSBURG, VA—FEBRUARY
http://www.worldquilt.com/wfw/wfwhome.htm
Also see:

• **COLONIAL WILLIAMSBURG**
http://www.history.org

• **WILLIAMSBURG AREA CONVENTION AND VISITORS BUREAU**
http://www.visitwilliamsburg.com

• **VIRGINIA QUILT SHOPS**
http://www.vcq.org/shops.htm

INDIANA HERITAGE QUILT SHOW
BLOOMINGTON, IN—LATE FEB–EARLY MARCH

WILLIAMSBURG AREA ATTRACTIONS, BY CAROL MILLER

If you fly in to Richmond or Norfolk to attend the quilt show, consider renting a car. While a shuttle will transport you to the four hotels hosting events, there is lots to do and see in the area—and nothing is in walking distance of the main hotel.

Near the hotel where the main quilt show is held is Busch Brewery—where spouses can have a tour and a taste.

If you go down Route 5 toward Richmond, there are about 5 old plantations—Shirley, Carter's Grove, Berkeley and some others. They vary in price and are quite nice. Berkeley's claim to fame is that it is where the first Thanksgiving was held (not, as you may have heard, in New England).

Down the road 15–20 minutes in the other direction is Jamestown, with both the actual archaeological dig and the reconstructed village. Yorktown is across the York River, site of Cornwallis' surrender at the end of the Revolution.

If the Civil War is your cup of tea, 45 minutes up I-64 brings you to Richmond where you'll find the White House of the Confederacy and several battlefield parks, as well as the Museum of the Confederacy, the Virginia Historical Society (with a spiffy new interactive history of Virginia display) and the Virginia Museum, which includes a spectacular display of Fabergé eggs from the Romanov Dynasty in Russia. The Valentine Museum is a house built around 1760 and has a large textile collection, including quilts. An appointment might get you a look.

A new improved museum dealing with Chimborazo Hospital (largest hospital in the world for battlefield treatment—during Civil War or ever) is in the works. The current one is on the actual site and has some of the worst and funniest films about history I have ever laughed through.

In the western part of the state, Harrisonburg houses the Virginia Quilt Museum. It is in an old house and usually has about 40-70 quilts on display.

—Carol Miller (**http://www.quiltuniversity.com**)

Richmond, VA

http://www.IHQS-Quiltshow.org

See also:

• ENJOY INDIANA
http://www.enjoyindiana.com

• THE INDIANA TRAVELER—REGIONAL TOURIST OFFICES AND INFORMATION LINKS
http://www.indianatraveler.com/tourism.htm

QUILT ODYSSEY
GETTYSBURG, PA—AUGUST
http://www.quiltodyssey.com

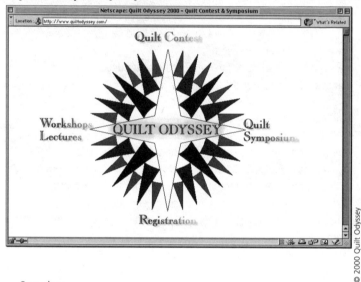

See also:

• GETTYSBURG
http://www.gettysburg.com

• GETTYSBURG ONLINE
http://www.gettysburgonline.com

• GETTYSBURG MARKETPLACE
http://www.gettysburgmarketplace.com

THE NATIONAL QUILTING ASSOCIATION, INC.
http://www.NQAQuilts.org

Coping with Repetitive Stress Injury On the Road and While Taking Classes.

Dian ("E/Less") Moore of Hummelstown, PA had surgery on both wrists because of carpal tunnel syndrome—a painful condition that can arise from the accumulation of small traumas or stresses to the body. Dian continues to travel and take quilting classes, but she prepares in advance and doesn't over-do. *"For at least a week before any event, such as attending the Quilter's Heritage Celebration in Lancaster, PA, I limit my computer work; I do no rotary cutting; and I do no cooking that involves chopping or cutting. When doing handwork while traveling in the car, I always use a wooden box to bring my work up close to me on my lap. Holding my shoulders back, and keeping my back and neck straight helps me alleviate pain and fatigue. I remember my pain pills, I take frequent breaks—stretching when possible—and I bring ice in a baggie to class, in case I need it, because I don't want to miss a thing."*

For more information on coping with repetitive stress injuries see:

• **TYPING INJURY FREQUENTLY ASKED QUESTIONS— THE RSI COMMUNITY'S ONLINE RESOURCE**
http://www.tifaq.com

• **COMPUTER RELATED REPETITIVE STRESS INJURY**
http://www.engr.unl.edu/ee/eeshop/rsi.html

An excellent book specifically for quilters is *RX for Quilters: Stitcher-Friendly Advice for Every Body* by Susan Delaney Mech, M.D., published by C&T Publishing (**http://www.ctpub.com**).

The NQA hosts its annual show in a different location each year. Check the site for details.

QUILTING IN THE TETONS
JACKSON HOLE, WY—OCTOBER
http://www.quiltthetetons.org

PACIFIC INTERNATIONAL QUILT FESTIVAL,
SANTA CLARA, CALIFORNIA—OCTOBER
http://www.worldquilt.com/piqf/piqfhome.htm

PENNSYLVANIA INTERNATIONAL QUILT
EXTRAVAGANZA, FORT WASHINGTON,
PENNSYLVANIA—SEPTEMBER
http://www.worldquilt.com/pnqe/pnqehome.htm

THE GREAT PACIFIC NORTHWEST QUILTFEST-
BIENNIAL CELEBRATION
SEATTLE, WA—AUGUST
http://www.apnq.org/ShoBro.html

WATERLOO COUNTRY & AREA QUILT FESTIVAL
WATERLOO COUNTY, CANADA—MAY
http://www.quiltfestivalcapital.com

CABOT QUILTING CONFERENCE IN THE UK
http://www.cabot-quilting.com
Conference dates and locations vary. Check the site for the latest information.

THE SYDNEY, AUSTRALIA QUILT FESTIVAL
SYDNEY (DARLING HARBOR), NSW—JUNE
http://www.ozemail.com.au/~quiltgld/festival.html

DALLAS QUILT SHOW
DALLAS, TX—MARCH
http://www.quiltersguildofdallas.org/QuiltCeleb.htm

NY QUILTS
TROY, NY—MAY
http://www.nyquilts.org

MINNESOTA QUILTERS QUILT SHOW
VARIOUS LOCATIONS, MN—JUNE
http://www.mnquilt.org/annual_shows.htm

ROCKOME GARDENS QUILT FESTIVAL
ARCOLA, IL—JUNE–JULY
http://www.rockome.com/Html/quilt/quiltshow.html

MAINE QUILTS
AUGUSTA, ME—JULY
http://www.MaineQuilts.org

SISTERS OUTDOOR QUILT SHOW
SISTERS, OREGON—JULY
http://www.stitchinpost.com/soqs.asp

free Guides to Museums and Galleries Featuring Quilts, Textiles, and Fine Art

Nothing beats a day at a museum where you can gaze upon work of arts in their full-sized, glorious, color-filled splendor. Being in the presence of a dazzling visual extravaganza warms the soul and propels an inner fire of creative thought. Museums feel good, they smell good, they humble, and they invigorate. This chapter includes Web sites for several such museums that all quilters should at some time visit. Many include information about present, past, and upcoming exhibitions, enticing images, compelling articles, educational materials, and other resources.

Free Guides to Quilt and Textile Museums

THE PEOPLE'S PLACE QUILT MUSEUM, LANCASTER, PA
http://www.ppquiltmuseum.com
The museum features Amish and Mennonite quilts, usually pre-1940, and other decorative arts.

THE FLORIDA QUILT COLLECTION FROM MUSEUM OF FLORIDA HISTORY, TALLAHASSEE, FL
http://dhr.dos.state.fl.us/museum/quilts

SAN JOSE MUSEUM OF QUILTS AND TEXTILES SAN JOSE, CA
http://www.sjquiltmuseum.org/index.htm

AMERICAN TEXTILE HISTORY MUSEUM, LOWELL, MA
http://www.athm.org/sites/athm24/home.html

THE MUSEUM OF THE AMERICAN QUILTERS SOCIETY, PADUCAH, KY
http://www.quiltmuseum.org

Tap into this site to learn what's new at the world's largest quilt museum, founded in 1991. You'll find information about upcoming exhibits and contests, workshops and events, tours, and the museum's extensive and exquisite quilt collection.

THE ROCKY MOUNTAIN QUILT MUSEUM, GOLDEN, CO
http://www.rmqm.org

THE INTERNATIONAL QUILT STUDY CENTER, LINCOLN, NE
http://www.ianr.unl.edu/quiltstudy
The center features the renowned antique and contemporary quilt collection of Robert and Ardis James and encourages the study of all aspects of quiltmaking. Online quilt conservation and storage information is included under the Education link.

THE NEW ENGLAND QUILT MUSEUM, LOWELL, MA
http://www.nequiltmuseum.org

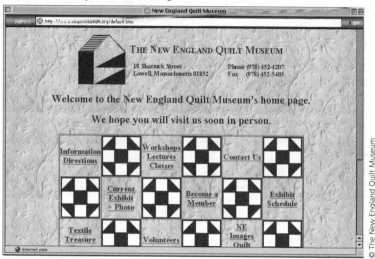

Celebrating America's quilting past and present, the New England Quilt Museum offers changing exhibits of contemporary, traditional, and antique quilts. The site features an exhibit schedule and a listing of workshops, classes, and lectures. Info on the Visitor's Bureau and other area attractions are included.

LA CONNER QUILT MUSEUM, WA
http://www.laconnerquilts.com

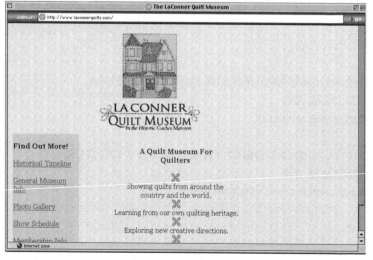

New shows featuring contemporary quilters and historical regional collections are offered every two to three months.

QUILTERS HALL OF FAME, MARION, IN
http://www.quiltershalloffame.org
Each July a celebration is held to induct a new honoree. Past inductees include Jinny Beyer, Nancy Crow, Yvonne Porcella, Karey Bresenhan, and Michael James.

LATIMER QUILT AND TEXTILE CENTER, TILLAMOOK, OR
http://www.oregoncoast.com/latimertextile

KENTUCKY MUSEUM QUILT COLLECTION, BOWLING GREEN, KY
http://www2.wku.edu/www/library/museum/quilts.htm

LAJOLLA FIBER ARTS, CA
http://www.lajollafiberarts.com

TEXTILE ARTS CENTRE, CHICAGO, IL
http://collaboratory.acns.nwu.edu/textilearts

THE MUSEUM FOR TEXTILES, TORONTO, CANADA
http://www.museumfortextiles.on.ca

NOVA SCOTIA MUSEUM— A FAMILY OF 25 MUSEUMS
http://museum.gov.ns.ca
Search "quilt" for a listing of museums with textile collections.

SELECTIONS FROM THE PETERBOROUGH CENTENNIAL MUSEUM QUILT COLLECTION, ONTARIO, CANADA
http://www.kawartha.net/~jleonard/qexhibit.htm

THE TEXTILE GALLERY, LONDON, UK
http://www.textile-art.com/tg1.html

THE AIDS MEMORIAL QUILT WEBSITE, SAN FRANCISCO, CA
http://www.aidsquilt.org

Over 13,000,000 persons visited the powerful and humbling AIDS Quilt that presently contains over 44,000 panels. An online searchable database allows you to view panels by name or by block number. Resources and details of the national display schedule are also available.

VIRGINIA QUILT MUSEUM, HARRISONBURG, VA
http://www.folkart.com/~latitude/museums/m_vqm.htm

> **TIP**
>
> Visit **Tourmobile** (**http://www.tourmobile.com**) for information on tours along the 25 major sites on and around the National Mall. **The Washington Metro Area Transit Authority** (**http://www.wmata.com**) offers a free guide to getting around the greater D.C. area with details on using the Metrorail system and locating points of interest.

THIRTEEN MOONS GALLERY— CONTEMPORARY ART QUILTS, SANTA FE, NM
http://www.thirteenmoonsgallery.com

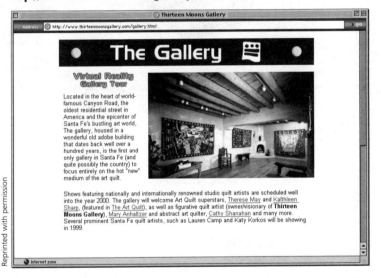

Reprinted with permission

Featuring the work of renowned studio art quiltmakers, take a virtual gallery tour, where you can travel through rooms and zoom in on the quilts. Entry information for upcoming shows is available.

FREE ONLINE QUILT AND TEXTILE GALLERIES

QUILTS AND QUILTMAKING IN AMERICA 1978–1996 FROM THE LIBRARY OF CONGRESS
http://memory.loc.gov/ammem/qlthtml/qlthome.html

THE PENNY NII COLLECTION
http://www.penny-nii.com
This virtual gallery connects you to private collections and special exhibits that can only be seen on the Web. View quilts of esteemed quiltmakers such as Michael James, Jane Sassaman, Therese May, and others in Resident Artists.

WEB MUSEUM NETWORK
http://sunsite.unc.edu/wm
Nicholas Pioch is the mastermind behind this ever-growing library containing images of thousands of paintings from Gothic style through the masters of the 20th century. You'll also find a special collection of over 100 images by Paul Cézanne and images from the calendar section of the Trés Riches Heures—the classic example of a medieval book of hours. Nicholas also offers an online guided historical tour of Paris and of the catacombs of Paris.

QUILTS, COUNTERPANES & THROWS
http://americanhistory.si.edu/quilts
18th century quilts from the Smithsonian National Museum of American History.

APPLIQUÉ MOLAS—
THE ART OF BEING KUNA
http://www.conexus.si.edu/kuna/eng/toc
View 32 pieces from the National Museum of the American Indian collection.

TO HONOR AND COMFORT:
NATIVE QUILTING TRADITIONS
http://www.conexus.si.edu/quilts2/toc

ART MUSEUM
http://www.artmuseum.net
This Web-based museum presents major exhibitions and art-related content—all for your perusal.

Free Guides to Museums in Washington, D.C. That Quilters Will Enjoy

THE NATIONAL GALLERY OF ART
http://www.nga.gov

THE NATIONAL MUSEUM OF WOMEN IN THE ARTS
http://wwww.nmwa.org

GUIDE TO WASHINGTON MUSEUMS
http://gwu.edu/~hannigan/guidetowashington

THE SMITHSONIAN INSTITUTION HOME PAGE
http://www.si.edu

THE TEXTILE MUSEUM
http://www.textilemuseum.org

Founded in 1925 by George Hewitt Myers, The Textile Museum is dedicated to furthering creative achievements in the textile arts. Tap into the site to view images and to learn about upcoming exhibitions, lectures, workshops, seminars, and demonstrations presented throughout the year.

In addition to The Textile Museum, Judy Smith of Washington, D.C. recommends visiting **Daughters of the American Revolution Museum (http://www.dar.org)**. *"They give private tours of their collection which holds over 350 historically significant quilts."* Judy also recommends scheduling a tour to see the Smithsonian's quilts, which are not open to the public. *"Private tours are given twice a month to groups of eight people at a time."* Visit **Smithsonian's Behind-The-Scenes Quilt Tours (http://www.si.edu/resource/faq/nmah/quiltour.htm)** for more information.

![icon] Free Directories to Museums and Galleries Throughout The World

WORLD WIDE ARTS RESOURCES
http://wwar.com

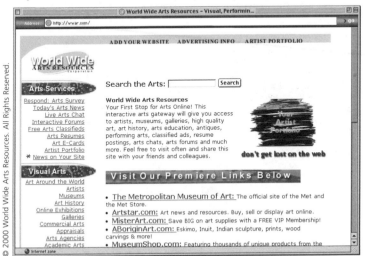

This is a must-bookmark portal to artists, museums, galleries, and more.

CRAFTS COUNCIL EXHIBITIONS (UK)
http://www.craftscouncil.org.uk/exhib.htm
Learn about the exhibitions at Britain's largest crafts gallery.

ART LOVERS GUIDE TO BRITAIN AND IRELAND
http://www.artguide.org/uk
Organized by artist, museum, and geography, the guide includes information to more than 650 museums and their related exhibitions.

MUSEUMS AROUND THE WORLD
http://archive.comlab.ox.ac.uk/other/museums/world.html
Jonathan Bowen maintains this collection of links to museums and galleries categorized by country.

ARTISANS' GALLERY
http://www.folkartisans.com/sup/resource.html

WORLD MUSEUMS AND GALLERIES
http://www.123world.com/museumsandgalleries/index.html

GALLERY GUIDE
http://www.gallery-guide.com

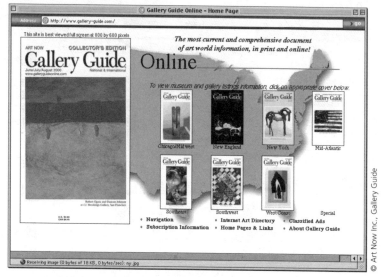

Art Now has been publishing Gallery Guide magazine for over 30 years. The Web site provides a plain text version of worldwide exhibition information taken from the printed guides, as well as a fully graphical Adobe Acrobat version of each guide published monthly.

MUSEUMS IN THE USA
http://www.museumca.org/usa/state.html
Maintained by John Burke, Chief Conservator at the Oakland Museum of California.

WHAT'S ON
http://www.embroiderersguild.org.uk/worldofembroidery/
   whatson.htm
A listing of UK and international embroidery and textile exhibitions and events, organized in date order.

INTERNET ARTRESOURCES
http://artresources.com
Information on galleries, artists, art-related articles, and over 1,184 museums in an alphabetized listing.

free Guides to Quilting Tours and Cruises

Ever dream about experiencing the textiles and crafts, foods and music, and cultures of a faraway land—all while being guided by a person who shares your passion for quiltmaking? How about taking a cruise on a luxury ship where between stops to exotic ports you can take quilting classes, eat scrumptious food, and lounge on a sun-lit deck while sipping colorful drinks from glasses with paper umbrellas. Sound too good to be true? Not so. Tours and cruises are available specifically for quiltmakers—some that can take you across country, some that can take you to other worlds.

Many quilting tours and cruises are not yet listed on individual Web sites but rather through a directory. A good place to start gathering ideas for what is available is by visiting Ann Anderson's directory to quilting tours and cruises at **QuiltWoman.com** (**http://www.quiltwoman.com/trip_fnd.cfm**).

 Free Guides to Quilting Tours

THE CRANSTON PRINT WORKS, WEBSTER, MA
http://www.cranstonvillage.com/mill
After taking a virtual tour of the Cranston Print Works mill, learn how you can take an actual tour of the Webster plant of the Cranston Print Works—the oldest textile printing company in America.

BEHIND THE SCENES QUILT TOURS
FROM THE SMITHSONIAN, WASHINGTON, DC
http://www.si.edu/resource/faq/nmah/quiltour.htm
Learn about bimonthly tours of the museum's quilt collection.

COUNTRY HERITAGE TOURS—
"THE QUILT TOUR COMPANY"
http://countryheritagetours.com

Textile designer and quilt collector Chere Brodsky is the founder of this company, devoted exclusively to quilt tours. The site details many exciting tours, such as an excursion through France that showcases Quilt Expo in Strassbourg and tours of Paris and Giverny.

QUILTER'S EXPRESS TOURS, ST. LOUIS, MO
http://www.maxpages.com/quilterstours

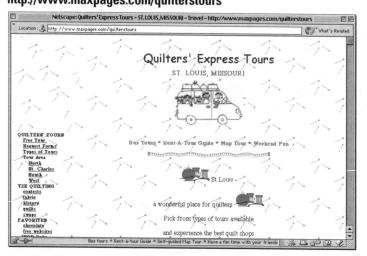

If you're planning a trip to St. Louis, visit this site for information on chartered bus tours, rent-a-tour guide, quilters' getaway, or a self-guided tour.

NANCY CROW—SOUTH AFRICA TOUR
http://www.nancycrow.com/HTML/southafrica.html

Learn about the arts, crafts, history, people, and cultures in rural, tribal, and urban areas on this tour to South Africa—the scenic beauty of which Nancy describes as "one of the world's best-kept secrets."

"I am often asked about the crime in South Africa. Yes, there is crime, but seemingly not on the scale of the USA. While we were there, South Africans thought it would be dangerous to come to the United States because of all the school shootings and wide ownership of guns. I felt as safe traveling in South Africa as I do while residing in the USA. Most South Africans are gentle. I believe the media and word-of-mouth hugely exaggerate all the negatives."

—Nancy Crow, Baltimore, Ohio

NANCY CROW—GUATEMALA TOUR
http://www.nancycrow.com/HTML/guatemala.html

This tour explores the textiles, art, crafts, people, history, and culture of Guatemala.

🛒 QUILTERS' EXPRESS TO JAPAN
http://www.QEJAPAN.com

Susan B. Faeder is an American quiltmaker who has lived in Japan, studied Japanese art and culture for over 30 years, and speaks fluent Japanese. Through her company, she offers tours to Japan that focus on learning about quilts and textiles within the context of Japanese culture.

🪡 TIPS FOR TRAVELING TO JAPAN, BY SUSAN B. FAEDER, NYC, NY

• Read a book—or two—or three. Try to read a little of this and that—a little history, some literature, some poetry—and then a guide book or two. A broad-based foundation is more important than learning the language.

• Get plenty of rest BEFORE the trip. Start a vitamin regimen 2-3 weeks before the departure date and try to have a regular schedule of sleep and exercise. You want to feel good and have as much energy as possible to enjoy your trip. Don't forget to have complete physical a few months before the trip and update your medications.

• Find two suitcases that "nestle" inside each other. About a week or two before the trip, start throwing things in one suitcase that you are thinking of taking. Then, each day take a few things out. When choosing articles of clothing for the journey, think in "layers." Don't worry about being in a fashion show. Pack sensibly. Two days before departure, you should have half as much as you started with. The empty suitcase you can fill with treasures (i.e., fabric!!) along the way to bring home.

• Take comfortable walking shoes—not NEW shoes—and preferably not tie shoes (unless you can bend over easily) as you will need to take your shoes on and off many times during your stay in Japan.

• Select a new journal and a new pen or colored pens or water colors. The trip moves very quickly and each day is packed with adventures, especially for us "visual people." Cameras are a must, of course, but it's nice to sit down at the end of the day (or in the middle of the night if you can't sleep) and go over your thoughts.

• Take along some of your favorite comfort foods (which must be sealed) like cereal bars, crackers, peanut butter, herbal tea bags, etc. The time difference is about 13 hours, and you may get hungry at odd times and need a pick-me-up.

• If you are taking film, take it out of the boxes, put it in a ziplock bag, and keep it in your carry-on bag. Before crossing through X-rays at the airport, pull the bag out and ask the attendant to take it around the X-ray machines. No matter what they say, the film will be different from all the exposure to the X-rays. Ditto on the way home.

• Take a small flashlight, a small calculator, and a small mirror.

• Take your money in travelers checks from a well-known company in U.S. dollars. These are easily exchanged for yen cash at any hotel lobby during the tour.

• Take a clean piece of white fabric—maybe up to a yard (bleached muslin is good), washed and ironed and stored in a large zip-loc bag. There are many places in Japan where you can get an imprint of a seal, called a "hanko," at no charge (or for a small fee). These beautiful, one-of-a-kind images serve as unique mementos and can be used later in a quilt. Typically, the ink provided for you will be orange or blue.

- Take a handful of photos that show your family, home, quilts, friends, and job. Pictures help when introducing yourself to other tour members. When you meet a Japanese person and are at a loss for words, a picture will speak for you and start the conversation.

- Don't agree to bring everyone you know a gift. This trip is for you. If you spend all your time searching for the perfect gift for 25 people, you will miss a lot of opportunities to do other things for yourself and with other tour members. Keep it simple. Don't make promises.

- When you board the plane, think: "JAPAN!" Look through your guidebook. Set your watch and your mental clock to the actual time in Japan and act accordingly: When your watch says bedtime, put on your mask and close your eyes. When the flight attendant says it's morning, try to eat breakfast.

- Drink plenty of water during the flight (whenever it's offered) and go to the bathroom frequently. Keep the body fluids moving as it will help a great deal to alleviate jet lag. Take frequent walks, stretch and bend; do yoga if you can—anything to keep your circulation moving will make it easier the first few days in Japan.

- When you arrive in Japan and get to the hotel, unpack, go for a walk, have dinner. Do not go to bed until it is at least 9:00 P.M.—if you can. This will help set your "Japan clock" in place for the next two weeks—so that you are not asleep in the middle of the day and awake all night.

- Finally, while on the tour, don't be late for the first activity for the day and try not to be the last one on the bus. Your fellow tour members will appreciate this.

TIP

Dan Youra's International Ferry Guide (**http://www.youra.com/ferry/index.html**) includes international, United States, and Washington State ferry service schedules. Dan also includes a large list of links to cruises, cruise lines, and tours.

Free Guides to Quilting and Other Cruises

"If you have ever wanted to go on a cruise, then treat yourself to a quilting cruise. If you allow yourself the pleasures of exploration, flexibility, and a fun-filled spirit, you will present yourself with a most incredible week of unusual experiences, joyful learning, great friendships, delicious food, and incredible scenery. As you return home, your mind will be filled to the brim with joyous memories."

—Joen Wolfrom, Bon Bluff Island, Washington

QUILT CRUISES WITH JOEN WOLFROM
http://www.mplx.com/joenwolfrom
http://www.mplx.com/quiltcelebration
Visit Joen's site to view photos of past cruises and learn about her upcoming cruise.

QUILT CRUISE WITH QUILT CAMP IN THE PINES
http://www.quiltcamp.com
Learn about the next quilting camp voyage.

"I recommend taking your spouse along on a quilting cruise. Mine had a great time—swimming, taking advantage of the exercise room—and each day we had breakfast, lunch, and dinner together. Classes are held while at sea, so you have the opportunity to check out the sites and side trips offered in each port.

—Norma McKone
(**http://people.delphi.com/battwoman**), Hardyville, VA

CRUISE LINE INTERNATIONAL ASSOCIATION
http://www.cruising.org
This cruise vacation planning site offers extensive links and information to all the major cruise lines.

CRUISE OPINION
http://www.cruiseopinion.com
Select a company and a particular ship. In addition to ship data, you can read an assortment of tell-it-like-it-is opinions from people who've traveled on it.

free Guides to Quilting Symposiums, Seminars, and Retreats

Imagine getting away from it all—kids, phones, bosses, underlings—to study quiltmaking for a glorious, uninterrupted weekend, week, or even two. Imagine large work areas, design walls, renowned teachers eager to share, and being surrounded by people interested only in creative pursuit. Sound good? It is. Quilting symposiums, seminars, and retreats offer such opportunity. I've had the pleasure of attending several over the years, and the experience is always uplifting and positive. Classes are encouraging and friendly, yet non-competitive. There is a palpable excitement that buzzes through the air as you and those around you learn new skills and share ideas. You emerge refreshed and ambitious—often eager to attend again.

Note that some seminars are held at colleges, meaning your stay is in a college dorm. If dorm life isn't for you (and I admit that it isn't for me), inquire about area hotels.

QUILT SURFACE DESIGN SYMPOSIUM
COLUMBUS, OH
http://www.qsds.com
Sponsored by Nancy Crow and Linda Fowler, SQDS is the largest symposium of its kind in the U.S. It offers two- and five-day sessions in June for all levels of quiltmakers, textile artists, and surface designers. Visit the site for class, teacher, and registration information.

 "Bring a pillow and make sure you bring all your medications—especially the prescription ones"
—Andi Stern, Chauncey, Ohio

QUILTING BY THE LAKE, MORRISVILLE, NY
http://www.quiltingbythelake.com

Classes for all levels of quiltmakers are held for one week late each July at SUNY (State University of New York), Morrisville Campus. The site includes class, teacher, and registration information.

"Bring a luggage carrier, pillow (especially if you're driving), and a clock-radio. The weather can range from terribly hot to quite cool—so be prepared for either extreme. There is a swimming pool that can be used in your spare time."
—Quilters from Albany, NY

"I've been to QBL several times and enjoyed it thoroughly each time. Two suggestions—take a fan and good walking shoes."
—Nancy Schlegel, Castleton, NY

NANCY CROW—BARN WORKSHOPS BALTIMORE, OH
http://www.nancycrow.com/HTML/barnworkshops.html
Hall of Fame quiltmaker and author Nancy Crow offers workshops each fall and spring taught by herself as well as other instructors on her farm east of Columbus, Ohio.

QUILTERS QUEST, MERCER ISLAND, WA
http://www.quiltersquest.com

Advanced quiltmaking and surface design classes are held for two weeks each spring, taught by two to three teachers—one always being renowned quiltmaker Nancy Crow.

QUILT CAMP IN THE PINES, FLAGSTAFF, AZ
http://www.quiltcamp.com

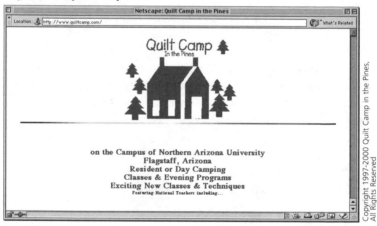

Dee Lynn and Audrey Waite are the directors of this camp held each year during the third week of July on the campus of Northern Arizona University.

THE ELLY SIENKIEWICZ APPLIQUÉ ACADEMY, WILLIAMSBURG, VA
http://www.ellysienkiewicz.com

Learn from one of the best appliqué teachers in the world. Elly's academy is held for four days each March.

QUILTING BY THE LAKE— AREA ATTRACTIONS, BY MARTY BOWNE, OWNER AND ORGANIZER OF QBL

• **Everson Museum of Art**, designed by I.M. Pei, has an outstanding collection of ceramic art from earliest times till today. Also displays other arts.

• **Salt City Museum and Fort**, a restored fort on the shore of Onondaga Lake with displays of salt making—one reason for the growth of Syracuse.

• **Erie Canal and Museum and Park**

For more information about the above attractions, visit Syracuse, NY Attractions (**http://www.syracuse.ny.us/ syrmayor/Activities/Features/home.html**).

• **Mansion House** (**http://www.oneidacommunity.org**) home of Oneida Ltd., the silver company. This originally was a Perfectionist Community in the late 1800s. Located in the Mansion House are the only know "braidings"—large and small framed pictorial images made by braiding silk. Very unusual. Call before going.

• **Green Lakes State Park**, Fayetteville (Finger Lakes Region) (**http://www.reserveamerica.com/usa/ny/gree**) includes an 18-hole Robert Trent Jones-designed golf course. Open to the public. There are also beaches, camping and picnic areas.

• **Strong Museum** (**http://www.strongmuseum.org**) about 120 miles away in Rochester, NY. Extensive doll collection. Victorian Village.

Also see **RoundTheBend's Upstate New York** (**http://www.roundthebend.com**) for more regional infor-

TIP

Learn about **ScrapFest**, a new quilting seminar to be held in the Blue Ridge Mountains (**http://www.nps.gov/blri**) community of western North Carolina, by visiting **Janet Wickell's Scrap Quilts** site (**http://www.scrapquilts.com**).

QUILTING BY THE SOUND, PORT TOWNSEND, WA
http://www.quiltingbythesound.com

Classes are held for all levels of quiltmakers during the last week in September at the Fort Worden Conference Center (with views of Olympic Mountains, Mt. Rainier, and the San Juan Islands). QBS also features a three-day pre-conference, complete with gourmet meals.

JINNY BEYER SEMINAR, HILTON HEAD ISLAND, SC
http://www.jinnybeyer.com/seminar/index.html

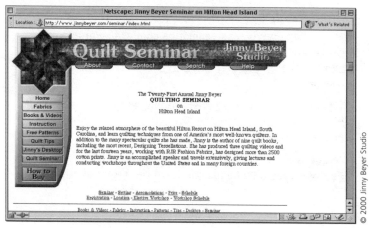

Learn quilting techniques from one of the world's most renowned quiltmakers. Late each January, Jinny teaches at the beautiful Hilton Resort.

🪡 QUILTING BY THE SOUND— AREA ATTRACTIONS, BY MARTY BOWNE, MERCER ISLAND, WASHINGTON

• **Seattle** offers many museums and galleries, the not-to-be-missed **Pike Street Market**, the Imax theater at the Aquarium, with a show of Mt. St. Helen's eruption, and much more. See **Seattle.net** (**http://www.seattle.net**) and Seattle.com (**http://www.seattle.com**) for details.

• **Victoria, BC** is about three hours away by ferry and car, and is home to **Buchart Gardens**, a must for gardeners and flower lovers. See **Visit Victoria British Columbia** (**http://www.visitvictoriabc.com/attract1.htm**) for more information about the Gardens and other area attractions.

• **Port Townsend** is filled with lots of charming Victorian homes, delightfully painted and with fascinating histories. You'll find many good book dealers and antique shops. Not the usual run-of-the-mill tourist town. The **Wood Boat Foundation**, a large boating community with many marinas and affiliated businesses, is also located in Port Townsend. See **Northwest Culture** (**http://www.nwculture.com**) and search small towns for Port Townsend information.

• **The La Conner Quilt Museum** (**http://www.laconnerquilts.com**) is located in La Conner, Washington. It's not open daily so check with the museum.

• Other places of interest include the **Olympic National Park** (**http://www.youra.com/olympic/olypark.html**) with good hiking trails and spectacular views, and the **San Juan Islands** (**http://www.guidetosanjuans.com**).

• For information on ferry service, see **Washington State and British Columbia Ferry Information** (**http://www.ferrytravel.com/index-1.htm**).

VERMONT QUILT INN
WITH JUDY DALES, GREENSBORO, VT
http://members.aol.com/jubda/quiltinn.html

Each fall, esteemed quiltmaker and author Judy Dales offers a four-day quilting class to 17 lucky students in the beautiful Highland Lodge, a country inn that was Judy's childhood home.

TRUDIE HUGHES QUILT CAMP, ELM GROVE, WI
http://trudiehughes.com/quilt_camp.htm
Popular quilt teacher and author Trudie Hughes offers a four-day quilt camp three times each year.

ALEGRE RETREAT—AN ART QUILTMAKERS RETREAT, SANTA FE, NM
http://www.katiepm.com/retreat.html
The 4 1/2 day retreat is held each March at the Sweeney Center. Always among the select group of teachers is the creator of the retreat, author and award-winning quiltmaker Katie Pasquini Masopust.

C&T PUBLISHING'S ANNUAL TEACHER'S RETREAT MORAGA, CALIFORNIA
http://www.ctpub.com
Well-known authors/quiltmakers conduct the Retreat sessions, focusing on sharing their expertise in organizing, promoting, and conducting successful classes.

🛒 TURTLE ART CAMPS
FROM TURTLE MOON STUDIOS, WOOSTER, OH
http://www.turtlemoon.com

Susan (Lucky) Shie and James Acord are gifted artists and sharing teachers. They offer five-day camps continually throughout the year. Visit the site to learn about the spirited atmosphere and flexible opportunities to learn appliqué, quilting, embroidery, embellishment, painting, drawing and more.

BLUE RIDGE MOUNTAINS OF VIRGINIA RETREAT, FLOYD, VA
http://members.aol.com/feedsack1/retreat.html

This quilting retreat is held each October at the Pine Tavern Lodge and Restaurant in the Blue Ridge Mountains of Virginia.

free Directories to Quilting Personalities and Their Teaching Schedules

What type of quilting teacher do you need? Maybe someone to offer gentle hand-holding and encouragement in settings where you can produce near-duplicates of the instructor's work. Maybe someone to inspire your artistic growth in a unique direction. But how do you learn of various teachers, what they offer, and their schedules? The Web, of course. This chapter includes sites that offer growing collections and databases of instructors. I also include individual sites of some notable quilt teachers, many of whom share invaluable travel insight.

Free Directories of Quilt Teachers

TEACHERS AND QUILT PERSONALITIES FROM SUSAN C. DRUDING AT ABOUT.COM
http://quilting.about.com/hobbies/quilting/msubpersonality.htm

QUILTING TEACHER LIST AROUND THE WORLD FROM SUSAN C. DRUDING AT ABOUT.COM
http://quilting.about.com/hobbies/quilting/library/bl_teachlistAL.htm

AUSTRALIA TEACHERS FROM DOWN UNDER QUILTS
http://www.duquilts.com.au/tutors.htm

TIP

If your favorite teacher authored a book, visit the Web site of the publisher. Many publishers such as **C&T** Publishing (**http://www.ctpub.com**) and **That Patchwork Place** (**http://www.patchwork.com**) offer information on their authors with links to their Web sites.

TEACHER SEARCH ENGINE FROM QUILTWOMAN.COM
http://www.quiltwoman.com/tchr_fnd.cfm

© 2000 Ann Anderson

Ann Anderson offers a searchable database of quilting teachers. Search by name, primary specialty, or geographic availability—or peruse the entire list of teachers. Be sure to register if you are a teacher; it's free and will spread the word of your services.

TEACHER REGISTRY FROM VCQ ONLINE
http://www.vcq.org/TeacherMain.htm
Carol Miller hosts this continually growing list of American and Canadian teachers.

AUTHORS AND TEACHERS FROM THE QUILT CHANNEL
http://www.quiltchannel.com/people/authors.htm

QUILTING TEACHERS FROM THE UK
http://www.quiltingdirectory.co.uk/tutors.htm

Web Sites of Notable Quilting Teachers

The following is a small sampling of the many esteemed quilt teachers available to teach you new skills. Visit their sites to learn about their work and their teaching schedules. Many teachers offer "extras" on their sites, such as free patterns and advice.

CHARLOTTE WARR ANDERSEN
http://www.charlottewarrandersen.com

ALEX ANDERSON
http://www.alexandersonquilts.com

© 2000 Alex Anderson

CHARLOTTE ANDERSON-SHEA
http://members.aol.com/CASInc/Char.html

JOYCE R. BECKER
http://www.joycerbecker.com

Looking for a particular teacher? Visit a major search engine such as Alta Vista (http://www.altavista.com) or Yahoo! (http://www.yahoo.com) and search on the teacher's name, surrounding the name with quotes. For example, to search for me, type <"Gloria Hansen">.

JINNY BEYER
http://www.jinnybeyer.com

People are amazed to learn that the awe-inspiring Jinny Beyer makes her exquisite quilts entirely by hand. Where does she find the time? By piecing while traveling, most often while on a plane.

"I always make sure to have plenty with me to work on. My worst nightmare is to get stranded somewhere and run out of sewing. Here's what I do:

1. I always have a hand-piecing project in progress.
2. Before going on a trip, I organize the pieces so that all I have to do is pull them out of a bag and start sewing.
3. I put my things in a sturdy plastic zip-lock bag, quart or gallon size, and individual blocks or pieces in smaller zip-lock bags.
My sewing kit contains:
• A package of needles
• A spool of conso thread (this is the large tube which has a hole in it the perfect size to fit a thimble)
• My wonderful little pair of fold-up scissors (no one ever questions your taking these on the plane)
• A small handful of pins.
When I'm ready to sew, I pull out my thread, put on the thimble that has been nestled in the hole on my finger, unfold the scissors, and start sewing. The thread is then perfect as a holder for the

scissors. I just stick the point down through the hole. That way you don't lose them in your lap or between the seats; and in case of turbulence, the points are thrust down inside the thread. The thread also makes a great pincushion—a no-no, but I have never had any trouble with the thread splitting, and I have everything right there."

—Jinny Beyer
Great Falls, Virginia

🛒 GEORGIA BONESTEEL
http://www.georgiabonesteel.com

PATRICIA B. CAMPBELL
http://www.patcampbell.com

SUSAN CARLSON
http://www.susancarlson.com

HOLLIS CHATELAIN
http://www.hollisart.com

KAREN COMBS
http://www.karencombs.com

NANCY CROW
http://www.nancycrow.com

JUDY B. DALES
http://members.aol.com/JUBDA

"I learned early on that you should never travel with more luggage than you can physically handle. Don't rely on a porter or luggage cart, because they are not always available. I make sure that all my suitcases have wheels and the extra ones piggyback on the two largest (one for each hand).

Always have a credit card with you. We tend to lose sight of our options when traveling because we are trying to be frugal. Whenever in a travel bind, that's the time to spend money—get a taxi, go to a hotel, buy a ticket back home—whatever you need to do to get yourself sorted out."

—Judy B. Dales
Kingwood, Texas

MIMI DIETRICH
http://www.mimidietrich.com

CAROL DOAK
http://quilt.com/Artists/CarolDoak/CarolDoak.html

ELLEN ANNE EDDY
http://hometown.aol.com/elleneddy/index.htm

ROBBI JOY EKLOW
http://homepage.interaccess.com/~eklow/index.html

CYNTHIA ENGLAND
http://www.englanddesign.com

ANN FAHL
http://www.execpc.com/~fahl/index.html

"I've invested in a good set of luggage on wheels that hooks together, so I can haul all of my personal stuff and teaching materials at one time. I prefer not to fold my quilts, but it is a necessary part of my work. I pack two short cardboard tubes in my suitcase (as long as will fit). When I arrive in my room, I unfold my quilts, place the tubes end to end, and roll the quilts around them. This helps smooth the fold lines and wrinkles from travel, and makes them look better when they get to the show or workshop. Packing a plastic garbage bag takes no extra space and will provide extra protection if you have to take them outside in the rain."

—Ann Fahl
Racine, Wisconsin

☒ CARYL BRYER FALLERT
http://www.bryerpatch.com

"Since I have been traveling full-time for over 30 years, I have learned to keep all my essentials in my carry-on bag—even when I'm at home. I have an extra set of cosmetics (in small containers), travel alarm clocks (two), vitamins, medications, etc., which never leave the carry-on suitcase. When I'm ready to travel, I go *through these supplies and replenish them. Since they never leave the suitcase, I won't risk forgetting to put them in. I also have a computerized list of all the supplies I could ever possibly need for any trip. I print it out the day before each trip, and check off each item as it goes into the suitcase."*

—Caryl Bryer Fallert
Oswego, IL

KAFFE FASSETT
http://www.kaffefassett.com

TRUDIE HUGHES
http://www.trudiehughes.com

🛒 MICKEY LAWLER
http://www.skydyes.com

GWEN MARSTON
http://www.keva.com/gmarston

MARIANNE FONS AND LIZ PORTER
http://www.fonsandporter.com/retreats.html

GAIL GARBER
http://www.GailGarberDesigns.com

MARY ELLEN HOPKINS
http://www.maryellenhopkins.com

MICHAEL JAMES
http://www.penny-nii.com/michael-james.html

🛒 MELODY JOHNSON
http://www.artfabrik.com

HELEN KELLEY
http://www.helenkelley-patchworks.com

JAN P. KRENTZ
http://home.att.net/~jpkrentz

KATIE PASQUINI MASOPUST
http://www.katiepm.com

GWEN MARSTON
http://www.keva.com/gmarston

JUDY MATHIESON
http://members.aol.com/judy4quilt

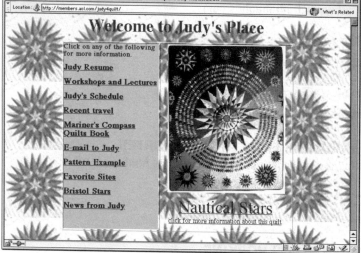

"*I pack all of the things I need to give a class in my small rol-laboard suitcase—including slides, teaching samples, master copies of my handouts, and my most important quilt. When traveling, be sure you include your name and address on the inside of your luggage (pin your card inside the lid) and have a destination address on the outside of your luggage in case it gets hung up and has to be delivered later.*"

—Judy Mathieson
Sebastopol, CA

SUE NICKELS
http://www.sue.nickels.com

YVONNE PORCELLA
http://sites.netscape.net/bporcella/home00

Netscape: Yvonne Porcella Studio Art Quilts

Netsite: http://sites.netscape.net/bporcella/home00   What's Related

Welcome To Yvonne's - Art Quilts - Porcella Studios

Contents:
  Home Page
  Information Center
    List of Lectures Available
    Classes/Workshops List
    Yvonne's Resume
  Art Gallery Center Hub
    Gallery Art Index
    Art Quilts - North Wing
    Art Quilts - East Wing
    Art Quilts - South Wing
    Art Quilts - West Wing
  Tour Center
    Photo Album - '98 Tour
  Guest Wing
    Links To Related Sites

Yvonne Working In Her Studio

© Yvonne Porcella

"I make small sample quilts that fit easily into a suitcase. These are easier to pack than a large quilt. I can easily carry six quilts in the 22" x 22" size range. I pack half of the quilt on the bottom of my carry-on suitcase, load my clothes, then fold the remaining half over the top of my clothes.

When teaching, I try to wear one of my patchwork vests which features the technique I am teaching. When making the vest, I piece the front side and also the inside surface. That way I can pack one vest and use it twice by wearing it inside and outside.

I spend a good deal of time ahead of time arranging the clothes I will carry with me. I prefer dark clothes to avoid getting stains on light colors. Each article of clothing has to be worn more than one time by rearranging tops with bottoms. This eliminates carrying too much. Conservation in packing is the key.

If I am teaching a class which requires kits or fabric painting supplies, I send boxes ahead of class time. In the negotiating, I arrange for someone to receive my boxes for me. The shipping costs are part of my materials fee."

—Yvonne Porcella
Modesto, California

DEIDRE SCHERER
http://www.dscherer.com

JOAN SCHULZE
http://www.joan-of-arts.com

ANITA SHACKELFORD
http://www.thimbleworks.com

SUSAN (LUCKY) SHIE AND JAMES ACORD
http://www.turtlemoon.com

"I put all our vitamins for each day into one film canister (the clear Fuji Film ones) and pack as many film canisters as days we'll be gone. We keep them as cool as possible, as our vitamins are natural.

Carry lots of extra goodies, such as a camera battery, film, tweezers (great for unsticking slides when lecturing), Band-Aids, safety pins, zip-lock bags, mini-stapler and staples, soap and shower cap, paper clips, Scotch tape, scrap paper, extra new toothbrush, etc. I pack as many pairs of scissors, sunglasses, and ink pens as I can take—they are always misplaced!

Using my computer, I make a travel itinerary, complete with all flight numbers, phone numbers, dates of arrival and departure, etc, and I give copies of this to our housemate, our family, and carry one with us, along with all needed maps."

—Susan (Lucky) Shie
Wooster, OH

AMI SIMMS
http://www.MalleryPress.com

DEANNA SPINGOLA
http://www.spingola.com

LORRAINE TORRENCE
http://www.lorrainetorrence.com

DAVID WALKER
http://w3.one.net/~davidxix

LAURA WASILOWSKI
http://www.artfabrik.com

RICKY TIMS
http://www.taqstudio.com

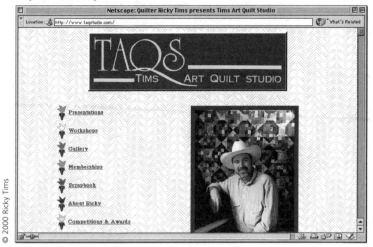

JOEN WOLFROM
http://www.mplx.com/joenwolfrom

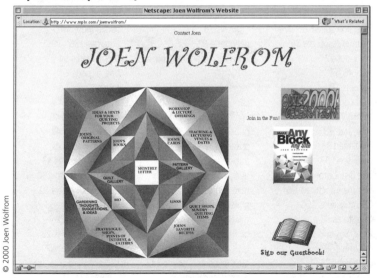

Be sure to visit Joen's Travelogue link for shops, points of interest, and eateries she's discovered during her travels.

INDEX

ABOUT THE AUTHOR

Gloria Hansen

is the author or co-author of 12 other Internet or computer-related books, including co-author of *The Quilter's Computer Companion*. Gloria is also an award-winning quiltmaker. Her work—often designed using a Macintosh computer—has appeared in numerous magazines, books, and on television. She has written for leading computer magazines (including *Family Circle* and *PC World*) and craft publications (including *Quilter's Newsletter Magazine, McCall's Quilting,* and *Art/Quilt Magazine*), and she writes the "High-Tech Quilting" column for *The Professional Quilter*. You can visit her Web page at **http://www.gloriahansen.com**. Gloria lives in East Windsor Township, New Jersey.

For more information on other fine books from C&T Publishing, write for a free catalog:

C&T Publishing, Inc.
P.O. Box 1456
Lafayette, CA 94549
(800) 284-1114

http://www.ctpub.com
e-mail: ctinfo@ctpub.com

FREE STUFF ON THE INTERNET SERIES

Frustrated with spending hours of valuable time surfing your way around the Internet? C&T Publishing's Free Stuff on the Internet Series helps you quickly find information on your favorite craft or hobby. Our Free Stuff guides make it easy to stay organized as you visit hundreds of sites that offer all kinds of free patterns, articles, e-mail advice, galleries, and more. This series of handy guides lets you explore the Internet's infinite possibilities.

Free Stuff for Stitchers

Includes Web pages for knitters, machine knitters, cross-stitchers, plastic canvas stitchers, beaders, tatters and other lacemakers, spinners, weavers, braiders, knotters, tasselers, and bowmakers. This book is the stitcher's guide to the Internet's infinite possibilities.

Free Stuff for Sewing Fanatics

Includes Web sites that offer free stuff for all kinds of sewing topics, including tailoring and fitting, sewing machine help, upholstery and draperies, home décor sewing, dollmaking, patterns and tutorials, heirloom vintage and bridal sewing, serging, fabric embellishment, and sewing for kids and pets.

Free Stuff for Quilters, 2nd Edition

The 2nd Edition of Free Stuff for Quilters includes over 150 updated new links on quilt patterns and tips, quilt discussion groups, guilds, and organizations, plus quilt shops to visit when you travel, how-tos for fabric dyeing, painting, stamping, photo transferring, and galleries of quilts, textiles, and fiber arts.

C&T PUBLISHING

www.ctpub.com